The
20th
CENTURY
in BITE-SIZED
CHUNKS

By the same authors

The Great Scientists in Bite-Sized Chunks

The
20th
CENTURY
in BITE-SIZED
CHUNKS

NICOLA CHALTON
& MEREDITH MACARDLE

Michael O'Mara Books Limited

First published in Great Britain in 2016
by Michael O'Mara Books Limited
9 Lion Yard
Tremadoc Road
London SW4 7NQ

A CIP catalogue record for this book is available from the British Library.

Papers used by Michael O'Mara Books Limited are natural, recyclable products
made from wood grown in sustainable forests. The manufacturing processes
conform to the environmental regulations of the country of origin.

ISBN: 978-1-78243-523-5 in hardback print format
ISBN: 978-1-78243-524-2 in ebook format

1 2 3 4 5 6 7 8 9 10

www.mombooks.com

Designed and typeset by K.DESIGN, Winscombe, Somerset
Maps by David Woodroffe

Printed and bound by CPI Group (UK) Ltd, Croydon, CR0 4YY

To my father, for giving us encouragement,
inspiration and guidance in the development
of this book, and in memory of my dear
mother, who helped me in so many ways.

Nicola Chalton

CONTENTS

LIST OF MAPS

INTRODUCTION

As the year 1900 arrived many people were still living as their ancestors had done for centuries. The global population stood at 1.5 billion and most people used coal or wood for fuel, grew their own food and inhabited small rural communities. The Industrial Revolution of the previous century had brought the benefits of artificial lighting and heating, steam trains, motor transport and the telephone, but only to a wealthy minority within the expanding Western countries.

Alliances between nations were primarily for military defence purposes. Colonialism allowed Western culture and technology to spread around the world – the beginning of the twentieth century's trend towards globalization – but it created unequal relationships between powerful nations and their colonies, which were exploited for raw materials and cheap labour.

Industrialized nations entered the twentieth century on a wave of optimism for the future. European countries dominated the world politically and economically. Their scientific and technological breakthroughs, coupled with the benefits of their empires, were promising them an ever-improving world.

At the turn of the century, only privileged men and even fewer women had voting rights, however, and women seldom had access to further education; children and young people did not have a voice; society had clear class divisions and racism was commonplace.

Much was to change in the twentieth century. No other century has seen such rapid and widespread developments, not just scientific and technological but also social, political, economic, medical and philosophical.

This book guides the reader through the complex events and developments of the twentieth century, helping to identify turning points and underlying causes and their effects, which have shaped our modern world. By the end of the century social, economic and political changes arising from the turbulent war years had caused the old world of aristocratically controlled kingdoms and empires to evolve into a new world dominated by international trade and trading alliances.

CHAPTER 1

OLD WORLD
SHAKE-UP

Europe's wealth had come from the Industrial Revolution and the colonization of overseas territories. Great Britain, the first nation to industrialize in the late eighteenth century, was the dominant colonial and trading power for much of the nineteenth century. British industrialization spread to Belgium and to the rest of continental Europe. Outside Europe, rapid industrialization of the United States followed the American Civil War (1861–5). Japan also adopted industrial methods from the West, centred around the railways, textiles and mining, in a bid to resist conquest by Western powers.

Textiles, steel, railways and other growing industries needed raw materials, including cotton, iron, rubber and oil, as well as markets for their products, leading many trading nations to take control of other countries as colonies. The wave of empire building of the late nineteenth century, driven by the urge to make profits and by rivalry between nations, was most developed in Britain, which had India as the centrepiece of its empire. By 1900 France, Portugal, the Netherlands and Russia had also developed significant colonial empires or territories over which they wielded political and economic power. Germany and Italy were emerging industrial powers in the process of establishing their own colonies, and Japan, with ambitions to expand commercially in China, was a growing economic and political force in Asia.

Industrialization created prosperous middle classes and vast labour forces, but not everyone shared in the economic prosperity of this period. At the beginning of the twentieth century, workers living in cramped, unsanitary dwellings and working long hours in dangerous conditions rebelled against their wealthy employers, demanding better working environments and higher living standards. In Russia, this was to lead to revolution, bringing down the tsarist Russian Empire.

In 1914 the First World War, the result of imperial rivalry in Europe, would shatter the peace that had allowed European expansion, bring down empires and replace old countries with new.

Flexing European Muscle

Western European powers had long had an interest in trade with Asia. Portuguese and then Dutch influence in Asia would be eclipsed by the British and French in the eighteenth century, with the British formally taking control of India from 1858, and the French controlling Polynesia from the 1840s and Indochina (Vietnam and Cambodia) from 1887.

The USA, founded by former colonies of Great Britain in 1783, was generally isolationist, preferring not to intervene in the affairs of other countries. However, it would annex the Pacific island group of Hawaii in 1898 for strategic military reasons, and take over the Spanish possessions of the Philippines and Guam in the Pacific and the Caribbean island of Puerto Rico following the Spanish-American War (1898).

Between 1878 and the outbreak of the First World War in 1914, European colonial empires grew rapidly as rival nations rushed to colonize the last remaining undeveloped parts of the world for their raw materials. The conquest of Africa was so competitive it was called the 'Scramble for Africa'. Besides commercial and economic benefits, the Europeans saw colonization as a noble enterprise guiding more primitive nations towards a civilized, Christian way of life. By 1914 Europe controlled 85 per cent of the earth's habitable land.

Scramble for Africa

The only continent still relatively uncolonized by the 1880s was Africa, the 'Dark Continent'. By then the prestige and economic, political and strategic benefits of controlling some of this vast land seemed tantalizingly within reach: vaccines had become available to combat tropical diseases, a much-feared threat to colonizers, and the invention of the Maxim machine gun promised easy victory in struggles with native populations. Instead of fighting each other, the European powers met at a Berlin conference (1884–5), engineered by German Chancellor Otto von Bismarck, and agreed how they would divide Africa among themselves.

By 1914, 90 per cent of Africa was under European control. Britain and France controlled the greatest areas of colonized land and the German Empire was the third largest beneficiary; Belgium, Portugal and Italy also held substantial territories. African colonies provided cheap labour, raw materials, gold (in southern Africa) and an open market for European goods, with a source of African

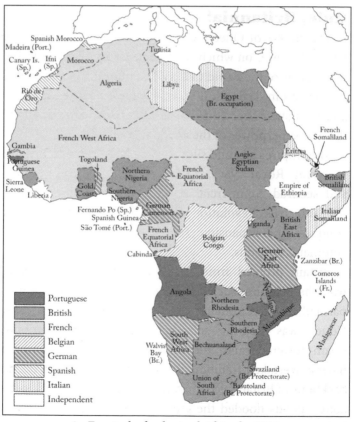

1. Europe had colonized Africa by 1914.

soldiers to fight in the world wars to come. The Suez Canal in Egypt was of particular strategic value, securing the flow of overseas trade between East and West. However, European partitioning of the African continent into new states, disregarding indigenous groups and overriding existing systems of African self-governance, was to build up trouble later in the century (see page 130).

Rule, Britannia!

In the course of Queen Victoria's reign (1837–1901), the British Empire, 'on which the sun never set', extended to so many parts of the world that at least one part of the empire was always in daylight. It was the largest empire in history and held sway over 20 per cent of the world's population: the first superpower of the modern era.

The empire's size and success were largely due to Britain's powerful Royal Navy, which dominated trade routes and secured commercial outposts, and Britain's lead in the Industrial Revolution, which provided the tools for conquest and expansion: the railway, the steamship and automatic weapons.

Britain profited from importing cheap raw materials from its colonies, such as sugar, tea and tobacco, and in particular, cotton from its former colonies in North America. Cotton was used for spinning and weaving in Britain's steam-powered mills, the manufacture of cotton fabrics having overtaken traditional woollens, which had been the backbone of Britain's economy since medieval times. Britain's cotton goods flooded the global market, undercutting less industrialized producers in India and Egypt.

The British Empire had also grown on the profits from trade in African slaves imported to America, until slavery was abolished in 1808 under pressure from the anti-slavery movement.

When Queen Victoria came to power, the empire was mercantilist (with tariffs designed to protect a favourable balance of trade, with exports higher than imports) and dominated by monopolistic trading corporations such as the East India Company. During Victoria's reign, Britain's economy transformed with the adoption of a policy of free trade (no tariffs, quotas or restrictions on imports or exports). The Victorians believed this was the key to prosperity.

The Kruger Telegram

During the 'Scramble for Africa', large deposits of gold ore were discovered in Transvaal, southern Africa, in the 1880s. The influx of British prospectors to the Johannesburg gold fields upset the Boers, the Afrikaans-speaking settlers of Dutch descent who had moved to Transvaal to escape British rule in nearby British-controlled Cape Colony.

Britain saw the Boer republic as a threat to its supremacy in the region and hatched a plan to overthrow the Transvaal government. The so-called Jameson Raid failed, provoking Kaiser Wilhelm II of Germany (a grandson of Queen Victoria) to send a telegram on 3 January 1896 to Transvaal President Paul Kruger, saying: 'I express to you my sincere congratulations that you and your people, without appealing to the help of friendly powers, have succeeded, by your own energetic action against the armed bands which invaded your country as disturbers of the peace, in restoring peace and in maintaining the independence of the country'.

The Kaiser's telegram inflamed tensions between Britain and Germany and reminded the British of the risks associated with their policy of 'splendid isolation' (fearing no enemies and needing no friends). Britain was to change its policy soon after, joining a system of alliances that would set Europe on a course for war.

Splendid Isolation No More

Britain suppressed the Boers in the Second Anglo-Boer War (1899–1902) and annexed their African republics, but the conflict had fuelled the growth of nationalism among Afrikaners, who resolved to win independence from Britain. Shaken by the conflict, Britain feared for the security of its empire, a serious issue because the empire was so vital to the British economy.

In 1902 Britain made a military alliance with Japan, by then the major native power in the Far East, designed to strengthen Britain's international influence and protect British trade in China. The alliance aimed to deal a blow at Russia, a rival of both countries: Russia had recently occupied Manchuria's strategic Port Arthur, threatening British commercial interests in China, and had ambitions in Korea, regarded as Japan's back yard. Britain and Japan could now count on each other's support in the event of a war with Russia or another power.

Britain also sought friendship with France, putting to rest long-standing disputes in a settlement called the Entente Cordiale (1904). The agreement provided mutual security for both countries in case of war in Europe, particularly against Germany, which was greatly strengthened since its unification under Prussian rule in 1871.

By 1910 Britain's manufacturing capacity had been eclipsed by that of the United States and Germany. In 1912 British Egypt was threatened by Italy's expansion into Libya (see page 14) and in a decade would be wrested from British control in the Egyptian Revolution of 1919–22. Although the British Empire would carry on expanding its territories until just after the First World War, Britain would no longer be the world's pre-eminent industrial and military power.

Imperial China Crumbles

One part of the world to escape direct colonial control by European powers was China. But Imperial China, a centre of civilization for at least two millennia and ruled by the Qing dynasty since 1644, was in decline. The Opium Wars (1839–42 and 1856–60), conflicts with Britain, which wanted freedom to continue the profitable but disruptive opium trade, had resulted in crippling reparations and the loss of the island of Hong Kong to Britain as compensation.

China had also suffered a bloody civil war (the Taiping Rebellion, 1850–64), loss of territory to Russia, conflict with France in Vietnam in the 1880s, and rivalry with Japan over Korea.

Europeans saw an opportunity for commercial exploitation but their rapid inroads into the empire were to lead to a violent reaction in the Boxer Rebellion of 1899–1901, led by members of a secret group, the Fists of Righteous Harmony (called 'the Boxers' by Westerners because of their style of fighting). The Boxers aimed to end Western influence in China, including Christian missionary work, which was seen to threaten China's ancient culture. In the words of a Chinese revolutionary: 'When I look at my country I cannot control my feelings. For not only has it the same autocracy as Russia but for 200 years we have been trampled upon by foreign barbarians.'

Violence erupted in the northern coastal province of Shandong, an area rapidly industrializing under German influence, when poorly paid Chinese workers joined the Boxers in murdering Europeans. In Beijing, the Boxers, who claimed supernatural protection from bullets, laid siege to the Legation Quarter where foreigners had sought refuge. When allied Western forces advanced to bring relief the Empress Dowager Cixi chose to support the peasant militia. It took fifty-five days for an international force of Russians, Japanese, Americans and Europeans to reach Beijing. The besieged foreigners were released and hundreds of Boxers were executed by the occupying forces.

The Empress was ordered to pay compensation to the foreign nations involved, crippling the Chinese economy. Thoroughly weakened, the Qing dynasty was to crumble in a revolutionary coup ten years later, bringing an end to Imperial China.

A Mobile, Consumerist New World

In 1900 Western society was reeling from a century of unprecedented change. Agrarian-based economies had been transformed by the Industrial Revolution: steam-powered engines replaced water and horse power and were now used in ships, trains and the first vehicles, with the very first modern (internal combustion engine) cars introduced around 1890. Spinning and weaving machines had transformed the textile industry. New processes had created wrought iron and steel products and developed coal mining. Roads had been improved and canals and railways had been built. The invention of the telephone and the telegraph had transformed communications.

Products of the enterprise culture included marvels of engineering such as the Suez Canal in eastern Egypt connecting the Mediterranean and the Red Sea and revolutionizing the flow of global trade by shortening routes between Europe, North Africa and Asia. Likewise the Panama Canal through the narrow strip of land linking North and South America (the Isthmus of Panama), constructed by the United States forty years later, between 1907 and 1914, improved sea transportation between the Atlantic and Pacific Oceans and became a vital conduit in international maritime trade. Ships heading to the US west coast no longer had to take the hazardous route around Cape Horn at the tip of South America.

The early twentieth century introduced a new era of mass-produced consumer goods, including those from the assembly lines at American Henry Ford's car factory. The innovation reduced production times for the Ford Model

T automobile, which by 1918 represented half of all cars in the USA. Affordable and marketed to the growing middle classes, Ford cars opened up the possibility of motor travel for Americans. The assembly-line breakthrough was soon applied to the manufacture of other consumer goods.

Through trade links and colonization, Western culture, science and technological advances spread around the world, affecting distant nations through a process of globalization.

First Powered Flight

In 1903 Orville Wright completed the first flight of a manned heavier-than-air powered controlled aircraft in North Carolina, USA, lasting twelve seconds. It was the culmination of years of experiments by brothers Orville and Wilbur. In 1909 French inventor and aviator Louis Blériot won a prize of £1,000 offered by the *Daily Mail* newspaper for flying a monoplane from England to France across the English Channel.

Before long the aeroplane was used in war missions, the first by Italians in the Italian–Turkish War (1911–12) for reconnaissance and bombing. By 1914, after the outbreak of the First World War, French pilot Roland Garros attached a fixed machine gun to the front of his plane, and in 1915 German fighter ace Kurt Wintgens scored the first aerial victory in a fighter plane armed with a machine gun synchronized to fire past the plane's propeller.

The Gilded Age

The industrializing nations, though economically powerful on the world stage, suffered internally from a divided society. Wealthy aristocrats and the middle classes benefited most from industrialization while the working class and poor were replaced by machines in factories or found new jobs working with machinery but with minimal wages. Their living standards remained low.

Europe's period of optimism, innovation, prosperity and stability, from the 1870s to 1914, became known as the 'Belle Époque'. During these golden years the wealthy classes enjoyed increased leisure and Paris became a centre for artists and writers. The natural organic shapes of the French capital's Art Nouveau style influenced architecture around the world. Literary realism, which found expression in authors like Émile Zola, was one of the precursors of Modernism (see page 29).

At the same time, post-Civil War America experienced the 'Gilded Age', an economic expansion stimulated by growth of the railways and new industries of petroleum refining, steel manufacturing and factory-produced commodities. Alongside America's new wealth came social problems associated with the vast labour force made up of migrants from rural areas and immigrants, many from European nations looking for better conditions. The social problems were said to be masked by a thin gilding of prosperity, an image captured by Mark Twain and his co-writer Charles Dudley Warner in *The Gilded Age: A Tale of Today* (1873).

Workers, Unite!

Unlike the USA, where the self-made man was recognized for his ability, Victorian society in Britain was built on a belief that inherited ownership of land was the mark of a gentleman, and the highest profession for a gentleman was in government not commerce. This divided the land-owning aristocrats from the commercial and working classes, and further division existed between the industrialist employers and the workers, who resented low wages and poor working conditions. Wealthy, religiously motivated philanthropists tried to resolve such difficulties with charitable works, but provision was erratic and there was little by way of a safety net provided by the state.

By 1910 Britain's economic growth had stalled, wages were stagnant and prices had increased, yet British workers were under pressure to increase productivity to maintain profit levels. Inspired by striking match-factory staff, gas workers and dockers, many joined labour unions for collective help, leading to a wave of strike action, the 'Great Unrest', whose aim was to improve the pay and conditions for working people. In 1926 Britain would have its first General Strike during an economic depression following the First World War, when striking British miners were joined in solidarity by other industry workers. A combination of middle-class volunteers, legal challenges and fearful union leaders led to the end of the strike.

The social inequalities associated with private enterprise and free-market capitalism provoked the growth of another movement, socialism. Where the labour movement aimed to improve conditions for workers within the capitalist system, socialists wanted to replace capitalism with a new system in which workers shared the ownership and control of the means of production. Allied with trade unionists, the European socialists spearheaded an international labour movement inspired by the slogan of German economist and revolutionary Karl Marx: 'workers of all countries, unite'. They demanded better conditions including an eight-hour working day.

Britain and other prosperous Western countries managed to contain the movements of the newly emerged mass working class during the precious few years of stability at the turn of the twentieth century, but for some nations these years were ones of impending or actual revolution.

Rumbles in Russia

The tsarist Russian Empire, stretching from Poland in the west to the Kamchatka peninsula in the far east of Asia, was the largest contiguous state in the world in 1900.

Russia's huge, diverse population included Germans and Asians, Russians, Poles and many other Slavic peoples – with so many nationalities there was constant political tension. Russian culture was imposed throughout the empire with priority given to Christianity, promoted by the Russian Orthodox Church. Russian Jews, like other minorities in Russia, were denied full rights. About 85 per cent of the population were peasants: emancipated from serfdom on Russian private estates in 1861, by the turn of the century they lived on the poorest land and in extreme poverty.

The empire had been slow to industrialize compared to imperial rivals Britain, France and Germany, but from 1892 infrastructure was developed, including the Trans-Siberian and Chinese Eastern railways. Foreign capital flowed in to finance new factories, and by the turn of the twentieth century Russia was the world's fourth-largest producer of steel and second-largest source of petroleum.

Rapid industrialization drew thousands of landless peasants into the cities, forming a new industrial working class. Living and working in harsh conditions (an average eleven-hour working day), they had no means to improve their lives: trade unions were illegal, strikes were prohibited and the Russian army quelled unrest. Revolutionary ideas spread through the working population.

Tsar Nicholas II ruled the empire from 1894. Marxist revolutionary and theorist Leon Trotsky from the Ukraine (then part of the Russian Empire) once remarked: 'Nicholas inherited from his ancestors not only a giant empire, but also a revolution. And they did not bequeath him one quality which would have made him capable of governing an empire, or even a country.'

The tsar gave his Minister of the Interior, Vyacheslav Plehve, the task of suppressing reformers and revolution-aries. Plehve claimed that 90 per cent of revolutionaries in Russia were Jews and encouraged mobs to make violent attacks on them (known as Jewish Pogroms), causing many Jews to leave Russia for the United States.

Plehve and the tsar saw an opportunity for expansion in the Chinese Empire, which had been rapidly declining ever since Japan defeated China in the First Sino-Japanese War (1894–5). Their targets of Manchuria, including the year-round operational Port Arthur in Liaodong Province,

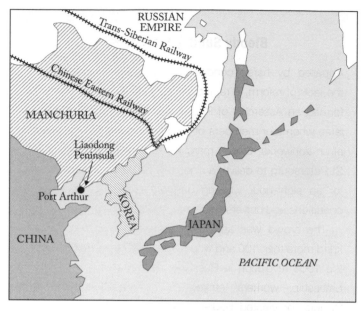

2. Imperial rivals: Russia and Japan.

and Korea provoked imperial rival Japan to retaliate in the Russo-Japanese War (1904–5), the first major war of the twentieth century. Japan's decisive victory confirmed its emergence as a powerful industrial nation while Tsar Nicholas was blamed for Russia's defeat. Russian revolutionaries resolved to act, notably the exiled Vladimir Lenin, who proclaimed in 1905: 'You are not alone, workers and peasants of Russia! If you succeed in overthrowing, crushing and destroying the tyrants of feudal, police-ridden landlord and tsarist Russia, your victory will serve as a signal for a world struggle against the tyranny of capital.'

Bloody Sunday Massacre

Appalled by harsh conditions in Russian factories and the lack of reform, a radical priest, Father Georgy Gapon, formed an Assembly of Russian Workers in 1903. A year later, when four members of the Assembly were dismissed at an ironworks, Gapon marched with 100,000 workers in St Petersburg to deliver a signed petition to the tsar calling for an eight-hour working day, higher wages, improved conditions and universal suffrage.

The crowd was attacked by the tsar's soldiers, who killed more than 100 and wounded 300. The event triggered the 1905 revolution in Russia: a mutiny on the *Potemkin* battleship, workers' strikes and the establishment of Soviets, or elected bodies of workers, in St Petersburg and other towns. Middle-class professionals joined in, establishing a Union of Unions and demanding a constituent assembly. Bowing to pressure, Nicholas II published the October Manifesto granting freedom of speech, assembly and association, no imprisonment without trial and the establishment of an elected legislative body, the Duma, to work towards reform.

In 1906 the tsar reneged on his agreement and dissolved the Duma, rendering the first revolution a failure, but seeds had been sown for future rebellion and the demise of the Russian Empire (see page 62).

Popular Revolts Spread

Dissatisfaction with corrupt autocratic rulers, repressive regimes and inequality stirred revolutionaries across the world.

The Mexican Revolution (1910–20), ousting dictator President Porfirio Díaz, who had been in office for thirty-one years, was sparked when Díaz fixed an election. The farming population of Mexico lived in poverty and saw no option but to revolt, plunging the country into years of violence and political instability.

The decrepit Persian Empire (territories of modern-day Iran), ruled by the extravagant and weak Mozaffar ad-Din Shah, experienced a revolution between 1905 and 1907. This led to a new constitution, the abdication of the shah and the establishment of a parliament in Persia. However, in 1907 the empire lost its autonomy when Britain and Russia concluded the Anglo-Russian Agreement, dividing Persia between them and solving years of rivalry in Central Asia, known as the Great Game, in which Britain viewed Russia as a threat to British India.

Anarchists, who aimed to destroy states and replace them with stateless societies, were also in operation in various countries, carrying out many individual acts of terrorism including the assassinations of King Umberto I of Italy in 1900 and US President William McKinley in 1901. The anarchists added violence and radicalism to the forces of popular dissent.

Revolutions in Art and Science

Scientific and technological advances that came about as a result of the Industrial Revolution encouraged artists to re-examine every aspect of life. A new movement, Modernism, grew out of Romanticism's nineteenth-century revolt against the effects of the transition to new manufacturing processes and bourgeois values. The Modernist artist was a revolutionary who eschewed traditional forms in art, which were seen to hinder progress. Working in France, Spanish avant-garde artist Pablo Picasso rejected traditional perspective and his experiments led to Cubism, involving the analysis and reassembling of objects in abstract form, and other diverse art movements such as Futurism and Surrealism. German Expressionist painters Paul Klee and Wassily Kandinsky, and Czech novelist Franz Kafka, reacted to the dehumanizing effects of urban industrialization and moved away from realism in the arts.

Modernism in music led Austrian-American composer Schönberg to experiment with traditional tonal harmony by using the twelve-tone technique, which avoids the limitation of using a particular key, a method that became widely influential among modern composers. In architecture, the Swiss-French Modernist Le Corbusier rejected traditional styles and reinvented buildings as 'machines for living in'.

Science continued to expand mankind's horizons in the early twentieth century. X-rays had just been discovered, by William Röntgen in 1895, and soon Marie and Pierre Curie were to identify radioactivity, leading to changes in ideas of the structure of matter. In 1900 Max Planck proposed that energy came not in a continuous flow (as previously thought) but in small packets or 'quanta', with a 'quantum' being the smallest possible amount. Einstein took up the idea in 1905 when he put forward his special theory of relativity, which overthrew the earlier view that space and time were absolute by saying they are relative to an observer (a million years to us may just be a few seconds for someone in a high-speed rocket). His general theory of relativity published in 1916 declared that matter causes space to curve, explaining the perceived movement of astronomical objects in the universe.

Nationalism Steers the Course of History

The Chinese and Russian empires were two of several imperial casualties in the first decades of the twentieth century. A force was growing that would destroy more empires in the First World War of 1914–18. In the comparatively peaceful climate of the nineteenth and early twentieth centuries, nationalism, an extreme form of patriotism, had served to unify the European nations, their populations confidently believing in the economic, cultural and military supremacy of their own countries. But it also created fierce competition and rivalry between European powers. The German Empire, created in 1871 with the unification of Germany following the Franco-Prussian War, had nationalist and imperial ambitions that would lead the world into the First World War, resulting in the collapse of the German Empire.

Other empires were to fall with Germany, including the Austro-Hungarian Empire in Central Europe, a nineteenth-century union of Austria and Hungary ruled by the Habsburg royal family, whose dynasty stretched back to the Holy Roman Empire.

The Ottoman Empire, originating in 1299 in Anatolia (modern-day Turkey), had taken over lands of the eastern half of the Roman Empire, the Byzantine Empire, in 1453. Its absolute ruler, the sultan, was regarded as the head of the Islamic faith by Muslims around the globe. The Ottomans' alliance with Germany in 1914, a bid to regain territory lost to European powers, was to seal the fate of this declining Eastern Mediterranean power.

CHAPTER 2

THE WAR TO END
ALL WARS

By 1914 the German Empire had become the dominant economic power in Europe, its chemical industry leading the world market. Germany had the biggest army in the world with a navy second only to Britain's, and was to play a decisive role in plunging the continent into the chaos of the First World War. But there were other factors at play across Europe, including pressures for democratization and socialism, nationalist demands, fear of the break-up of hard-won empires, and, crucially, fear of other nations. Germany feared encirclement by France and Russia; Russia was concerned about the potential for German control over the Balkans and the Near East; France, crushed by its defeat in the Franco-Prussian War (1870–1), felt threatened by Germany's growing strength; and Britain was worried about losing its dominant place in the world.

Fear pushed the nations into a war they believed to be necessary and justified for securing their respective freedoms. They expected the war to be over in a few heroic months and that it would put an end to all wars. In fact, it was the beginning of a new kind of total war involving the mobilization of civilians at home, a war in which technology was to become unprecedentedly important and destructive, and a war that would lead to yet more conflict.

Drift to War

In the decade before the event that would light the First World War's fuse, the imperialistic countries of Europe had jostled for power and status, competing over trade, markets and territory for economic self-interest. While Germany was rising, the Ottoman and Austro-Hungarian empires were declining. Britain still had the largest naval fleet in the world and built HMS *Dreadnought* (1906) and other battleships to maintain its naval supremacy. Other nations, especially Germany, raced to build heavy-calibre guns and to extend their armies, believing that these would act as deterrents to war.

In light of the escalating arms race and struggling with spiralling expenditure, Russia's Tsar Nicholas II initiated a peace conference at The Hague in 1899 that aimed to negotiate disarmament and to force countries to settle international disputes through arbitration rather than war. But the initiative was vetoed by Germany. A second peace conference, called by US President Theodore Roosevelt in 1907, brought in some rules of war, but an attempt to limit armaments, seen by Germany as a British move to restrict the German naval fleet, was thrown out.

Leaders grew complacent about the possibility of war. They believed they could maintain a balance of power and protect themselves from conflict through contractual alliances. But these very alliances entangled Europe in a mesh of potentially burdensome obligations that became a major cause of the First World War.

The World Is a Tinderbox

By 1907 growing rivalries had divided the powers into two groups: on one side the Triple Alliance of Germany, Austria-Hungary and Italy; on the other, the Triple Entente of Russia, Britain and France. The cause of this division stemmed partly from the Franco-Prussian War of 1870–1, which had left France and Germany bitterly opposed, and partly from rivalries in the Balkan region.

The Balkans, the multi-ethnic south-eastern peninsula of Europe once part of the Orthodox Christian Eastern Roman Empire (the Byzantine Empire), had been controlled by the Muslim Ottoman Empire since the Middle Ages. Over two centuries Russia had gradually extended southwards into Ottoman territory, siding with the Orthodox Christian Serbs and pledging to come to Serbia's aid in a crisis. Serbia and Greece had broken free of Ottoman rule in the nineteenth century, and during the Russo-Turkish War of 1877–8 Russia had headed an Eastern Orthodox coalition of Balkan states against the Ottoman Empire, fighting to end discrimination against Christians: their mission had earned independence for Montenegro, Romania and part of Bulgaria.

In the early twentieth century Russia continued to support Balkan independence and was particularly galled by the annexation of Bosnia-Herzegovina from the Ottoman Empire by Russia's arch-rival Austria-Hungary in 1908.

The German Chancellor and architect of Germany's unification, Otto von Bismarck, expected France to attempt recovery of Alsace-Lorraine, which had been ceded to Germany after the Franco-Prussian War, and so formed an alliance with Russia and Austria-Hungary in 1873. The treaty was short-lived due to tensions between Russia and Austria-Hungary over Bosnia-Herzegovina. Their rivalry led to a second alliance between Germany and Austria-Hungary in 1879, joined by Italy in 1882 as the Triple Alliance, the members promising mutual support in the event of an attack by another great power. The powerful Triple Alliance precipitated a defensive Franco-Russian alliance in 1894.

Compounding the tangle of mutual defence treaties was a change in German foreign policy in the 1890s following Chancellor Bismarck's resignation over disagreements with the German emperor, Kaiser Wilhelm II. Bismarck's departure set the empire on a new course influenced by the Kaiser's conviction that European powers were plotting to encircle his country and stop Germany from expanding. Germany's erratic new policy provoked Britain to form alliances with its colonial rivals, France (in the Entente Cordiale of 1904) and Russia (in 1907).

Mounting tensions erupted in the Balkan Wars of 1912–13. Greece, Serbia and Bulgaria, already independent from the Ottoman Empire, annexed Ottoman-controlled Macedonia in order to free more Slavic people from Ottman rule. Bosnian Serbs of Bosnia-Herzegovina, controlled by Austria-Hungary, now clamoured for the freedom to join a greater Serbia.

What happened next had been predicted by Bismarck years earlier when he announced: 'One day the great European War will come out of some damned foolish thing in the Balkans.'

The Balkan Spark

On 28 June 1914 Austria's heir apparent, Archduke Franz Ferdinand, was assassinated in the Bosnian capital of Sarajevo by a Serbian nationalist. The archduke had come to inspect Austrian imperial soldiers in Bosnia-Herzegovina, annexed by Austria six years earlier. The day he and his wife toured the city in an open car coincided with St Vitus' Day, when ethnic Serbs remember Serbian martyrs who fell during the Battle of Kosovo in 1389 against the Ottoman Empire. A secret Serbian nationalist group, the Black Hand, which wanted independence for Bosnia, chose this special day to act against imperial Austria. When one of the revolutionaries threw a bomb at the archduke's car, it rolled off the back leaving the imperial couple unharmed, but later, when the procession took a wrong turn, another member, nineteen-year-old Bosnian-Serb Gavrilo Princip, shot dead Franz Ferdinand and his wife.

Austria-Hungary blamed the Serbian government for the assassination and issued an ultimatum, calling on Serbia to suppress anti-Austrian activities. Serbia agreed to most of Austria's demands but on 28 July 1914 Austria, fortified by Germany's unconditional promise of support if Russia intervened, declared war on Serbia. What could have been a small conflict then snowballed into the Great War as a result of the mutual defence treaties.

An Unstoppable War

The day after declaring war, Austria bombarded the Serbian capital of Belgrade. Russia mobilized its troops in defence of Serbia.

Kaiser Wilhelm II, who had craved power and authority in world affairs for Germany, now shrank from the prospect of going to war on two fronts: against Russia and its ally France, supported by England. But instead of offering autonomy for Alsace in exchange for France remaining neutral, which might have limited the conflict, Germany sent France an ultimatum not only demanding that France remain neutral but also offering as a guarantee of neutrality the strategic fortresses of Toul and Verdun for the duration of armed conflict. France replied that it 'would act in accordance with her interests'. England then offered to keep France neutral if Germany promised to stay neutral against France and Russia; the offer was misunderstood in the course of a telephone conversation between the English Foreign Secretary and the German Ambassador in London to be that France would be kept neutral if Germany went to war against only Russia.

Hoping for a war on just one front, the Kaiser tried to stop the mobilization of German troops westwards towards France, but on 1 August 1914 the German General von Moltke told the Kaiser that to change arrangements would reduce the army to a 'chaotic rabble'. The same day, German troops crossed the frontier into Luxembourg and Germany presented its declaration of war to Russia.

The German military commanders were following a long-held military plan, the Schlieffen Plan, to outflank the French armies by going round them, via Belgium, and capture Paris within six weeks, thereby ending the threat in the west before turning to attack Russia. The plan assumed Russia would be slow to mobilize its huge army and Britain would not send troops in time to assist France.

But when Germany attacked Belgium, after being refused free passage for its troops through their country, and declared war on France (3 August), Britain, in keeping with an 1839 treaty promising to protect Belgian neutrality, declared war on Germany on 4 August. The astonished German Chancellor, Bethmann-Hollweg, exclaimed, 'For a scrap of paper, Great Britain is going to make war?'

Russia also surprised the Germans by taking just ten days to mobilize, forcing Moltke to divide his army and send troops east as well as west.

The British Foreign Secretary, Sir Edward Grey, seeing that war would soon engulf the continent, commented: 'The lamps are going out all over Europe. We shall not see them lit again in our lifetime.'

The Two Camps

As war erupted the world lined up into two hostile camps. Germany and Austria-Hungary formed the core Central Powers. Italy, under the terms of the Triple Alliance, was obliged to join them only in a defensive war and chose to remain neutral at the outset. During the frantic diplomatic crisis of July 1914, in which Germany attempted to destabilize British control of India by inciting a rebellion there, the Ottoman Empire (Turkey) signed up with the Central Powers. The Ottomans controlled the Turkish

3. *Europe's military alliances during the First World War (1914–18).*

Allied powers (Romania joined 1916; Greece joined 1917)

Central powers (Bulgaria joined 1915)

Neutral

Straits and access to the Black Sea and could potentially cut Russia off from its British and French allies and southern supplies. Bulgaria in the Balkans enjoyed similar strategic advantages and joined the Central Powers in 1915.

On the opposing side, the Allied Powers at the beginning of the war were members of the Triple Entente – France, Britain, Russia and their colonies, along with Serbia. Japan, Britain's ally since 1902, joined the Allies in August 1914, promptly helping to destroy German ships around China and occupying German territories in the Far East. Italy would join the Allies in April 1915, wooed by assurances of Austro-Hungarian territory on Italy's border. Romania joined the Allies in August 1916. The United States tried to remain neutral but entered the war in April 1917 on the side of the Allies (see page 49). Greece joined the Allies in July 1917. For the first time in history the conflict would be global, affecting every continent.

Your Country Needs You!

Men flocked to fight for their country and professional armies rapidly expanded. Britain, unlike France, Germany, Russia and Austria-Hungary, had no compulsory enlistment (military draft) so relied on volunteers. 'Your Country Needs YOU!' was the slogan on the famous poster featuring Britain's Secretary of State for War, Lord Kitchener, who encouraged more than a million enthusiastic young men to join Britain's expeditionary force. Many were unprepared for battle and their 'Pals' battalions, swollen with friends and neighbours, suffered high casualties. To maintain enlistment targets, Britain introduced conscription in 1916 for all men aged eighteen to forty-one (up to fifty-one in the last months of the war).

The French and British empires enlisted Africans and Indians to fight for the Allies, and the British dominions of Australia, Canada, New Zealand and South Africa recruited their own forces to support the Allies. In 1917 US President Woodrow Wilson reintroduced the military draft in the United States.

Conscription applied only to male citizens but many women joined up as volunteer nurses, ambulance drivers and war doctors. Women at home took jobs vacated by men or new jobs in munitions factories; others supported the war effort through charitable work.

The Western Front

The struggle that would decide the course of history was fought on many fronts but in particular the Western Front, in France and northern Belgium (Flanders). This main theatre of war was established during the first few months of the conflict.

German troops advancing through Belgium met stiff resistance and in fighting their way towards the French border brutally killed more than 6,000 Belgian civilians. For the advancing German armies, every civilian was a potential threat; villages were burned out and executions of civilians and priests were ordered to instil fear in Germany's enemies.

The Germans first encountered the Allies on 23 August 1914: the British Expeditionary Force at Mons in Belgium, close to the French border. Numerically superior, the German army forced the British to retreat to the Marne River east of Paris.

Battle of the Marne

The German advance had come within 50 kilometres (30 miles) of Paris, prompting the French government to leave the capital. French reconnaissance pilots spotted forces of German General Alexander von Kluck abandoning the Schlieffen Plan to head east instead of west around Paris, as they pursued retreating Allied forces towards the Marne River. A gap developed between Germany's First and Second Armies and French commander Joseph Joffre seized the opportunity to counter-attack with the Allied Sixth Army on 5 September 1914, striking the right flank of von Kluck's forces. French reserves from the eastern front at Lorraine were rushed by rail to Paris and then to the front in taxis to reinforce the Sixth Army and help push the Germans northwards. After a week of heavy fighting the Germans dug in around the Aisne River.

The first major battle of the war had stopped Germany's advance and saved Paris but claimed more than 300,000 casualties, a scale not seen before in warfare. For the next two months both sides attempted to outflank each other in a series of battles fought closer and closer to the North Sea. This 'Race to the Sea' created a 640-kilometre (400-mile) network of defensive trenches between Flanders' coast and (neutral) Switzerland, where the conflict would reach a four-year stalemate on the Western Front.

Fields of Flanders

The 'Race to the Sea' culminated in the devastating First Battle of Ypres in western Flanders (north-west Belgium), between 19 October and 22 November 1914. Both sides dug themselves into lines of trenches facing each other, divided by barbed wire and a narrow strip of 'no man's land'. Soldiers defended their positions, launched offensives, and ate and slept in appalling conditions of mud, lice, rats and freezing weather, at risk of sniper fire, shells and trench raids. Each side tried to advance past the other, while artillery and machine guns dominated the battlefield, which became littered with the dead. British, French and Belgian troops, though outnumbered, succeeded in halting the German advance towards the English Channel ports, so vital for maintaining supplies to France and Belgium through the war.

By November 1914 all armies had lost morale. Failure to break the deadlock meant the war would not be over by Christmas, as everyone had hoped. There was a short reprieve: on Christmas Day, Western Front soldiers on both sides spontaneously made a truce, climbed out of their trenches, played football and socialized in the wilderness of the battlefield.

Ypres became the centre of sustained battles. In the Second Battle of Ypres (22 April to 25 May 1915) the Germans used toxic chlorine gas against French colonial and Canadian troops. The gas, blown by the wind and penetrating the trenches, had a devastating effect, prompting the Allies to develop their own chemical weapons and gas masks.

The more lethal mustard gas was used by the Germans in the Third Battle of Ypres (the Battle of Passchendaele), from July to November 1917, the longest and most costly of Flanders' battles in terms of casualties, fought in a swamp of mud caused by heavy August rainfall. Under British commander Douglas Haig, British and Canadian forces occupied the ruined village of Passchendaele near Ypres, a small gain for casualties on both sides totalling more than 850,000.

A Canadian soldier-poet, John McCrae (1872–1918), wrote:

> *In Flanders fields the poppies blow*
> *Between the crosses, row on row,*
> *That mark our place; and in the sky*
> *The larks, still bravely singing, fly.*
> *Scarce heard amid the guns below.*

Eastern and Southern Fronts

Unlike the Western Front, the war on the Eastern Front did not become bogged down in static trench warfare. The Russians crossed the German border into East Prussia on 17 August 1914, meeting a smaller German army at Tannenberg. The skilled German troops virtually destroyed the entire Russian Second Army on 26 August, leading to the surrender of 90,000 Russian soldiers, the suicide of Russian general Alexander Samsonov and a massive boost for German morale.

Further south, in Galicia, the Russians fared better, overwhelming the Austrian forces by 3 September. Like the Germans, the Russians became known for brutal attacks on civilians, many of whom fled as their forces advanced. The large population of Jews in Galicia suffered appalling violence at the hands of the troops.

The Central Powers became ever more dependent on Germany, which inflicted serious defeats on the Russians early in 1915, in East Prussia, Poland, part of Latvia and Lithuania. The Germans wrested Galicia from the Russians by the summer, and by autumn 1915 the Central Powers had taken Serbia, securing a land supply route between the Ottoman Empire and Germany.

Italy joined the Allies in May 1915 but Austria managed to keep the Italians at bay to the south. However, the Austro-Hungarian front crumbled in June 1916 under an assault by Russian General Aleksey Alekseyevich Brusilov in Belarus, the Ukraine and Romania. There were huge losses on both sides and Romania was drawn into the war on the side of the Allies. In October 1917 Italy suffered a disaster at the Battle of Caporetto against Austrian and German forces, and was humiliated at the end of the war when earlier promises of territory on its border with Austria-Hungary were not honoured (see page 72).

Misadventure at Gallipoli

In March 1915, to counter the stalemate on the Western Front, Britain's First Lord of the Admiralty, Winston Churchill, proposed to attack the Ottoman Empire (Turkey), which had sided with Germany and Austria in 1914. The Gallipoli Campaign (1914–16) took place on the strategic Gallipoli peninsula in eastern Turkey, with the aim of capturing the Turkish capital of Constantinople. However,

British and French warships entering the Dardanelles strait were sunk in a minefield. The land invasion by Australian, New Zealand, Indian, French and Senegalese troops reached a stalemate against an impregnable Turkish defence, heroically led by Mustafa Kemal Atatürk. It was a disaster for the Allies, whose forces were evacuated by January 2016. Churchill lost his government position soon after, though he would rise again years later to lead Britain through the Second World War. For the Ottoman Turks, the victory formed a basis for the emergence of modern Turkey under Atatürk after the close of the war (see page 60).

Arab Revolt

More successful for the British was the destabilization of the Ottoman Empire in its Arab lands of the Middle East. The Arab Revolt from June 1916 to 1918, encouraged by the British in return for a promise of Arab independence after the war, was led by Prince Faisal of the Hashemite clan with rebels trained in guerrilla warfare by British intelligence officer T. E. Lawrence ('Lawrence of Arabia'), who had won the trust of the Arabs. The camel-mounted forces carried out sabotage attacks on railways and captured the port of Aqaba in July 1917. In December 1917 the holy city of Jerusalem fell to the British under General Edmund Allenby, and Damascus fell to the Allies in October 1918, ending the war in the Middle East. But instead of supporting Faisal in an independent Arab state, the British and French split the Middle East between themselves: Palestine and Jordan went to the British and Syria and Lebanon to the French. As a small compensation, Faisal was made king of Iraq.

The unfulfilled promise of an independent Arab state and Britain's later promise to make a homeland in Palestine for the Jews would lie at the root of the Arab–Israeli conflict later in the century (see page 149).

Vive La France!

By 1916 the Central Powers had strengthened their position and planned to force a victory in the west with a massive assault on the French fortress city of Verdun, about 200 kilometres (124 miles) east of Paris. The attack began with a huge artillery bombardment on 21 February 1916, using 1,200 German heavy guns and vast quantities of shells. The German infantry swept forward, crossing the shallow French trenches to take Fort Douaumont on 24 February. But instead of withdrawing from Verdun, the French halted the German advance, their fight symbolizing a battle for France itself. Reinforcements and supplies were brought to French troops along a single road, the Voie Sacrée (Sacred Road), fuelling repeated attacks and counter-attacks. Finally, the French regained lost ground in October 1916. The patriotic battle to save France came at a high price – around 700,000 Franco-German casualties.

Hell Let Loose

In the same year, to relieve pressure on the French at Verdun, British and Dominion troops led an attack at the Somme River in northern France, which was largely the plan of British commander Douglas Haig. For eight days from 23 June 1916, the Allies pounded the German line using more than 2,000 guns, and on 1 July British and

Commonwealth infantry went 'over the top' in an assault on enemy trenches. However, the Germans emerged from deep dugouts to mow the advancing soldiers down with machine-gun fire. The fighting continued over months, both sides using poison gas and the British deploying the first tanks. By November 1916 small Allied territorial gains of around 12 kilometres (7 miles) had come at the cost of more than a million killed or wounded. It was the worst battle of the war in terms of losses for so little gain.

War at Sea

The Allies relied on their command of the sea to ship supplies and troops. Although the war was largely fought on land, Germany attempted to challenge British naval supremacy in the Battle of Jutland (May 1916). This clash of big-gun battleships in the North Sea was a strategic British victory that left the German Navy severely diminished.

From February 1915 German submarines (U-boats) had been ordered to attack merchant shipping in retaliation for a British naval blockade in the North Sea that was stopping supplies from reaching Germany. The Allies lost many ships through U-boat attacks but eventually neutralized the threat by placing merchant ships among defended convoys and by developing anti-submarine warfare, including depth-charges and hydrophone equipment to detect U-boats underwater.

Civilian deaths caused by U-boat attacks provoked international hatred towards Germany and were largely responsible for America joining the war.

Lusitania and Zimmerman

On 7 May 1915 a German submarine attacked the Royal Mail Ship *Lusitania*, a British ocean liner en route from New York to Liverpool, England, carrying supplies for Britain and 1,900 passengers. Germany claimed the ship was also carrying arms. The torpedo strike sunk the ship and 128 of the 1,200 passengers lost were American. A public outcry in America led to pressure on Germany to halt the attacks. However, in 1917, frustrated by the deadlock on the Western Front, Germany reintroduced indiscriminate U-boat attacks, a decision that further hardened American public opinion towards Germany.

America was again outraged in January 1917 when British intelligence intercepted the Zimmerman Note from Germany to Mexico, proposing a military alliance between the two countries in the event of the United States entering the war, with a promise of Mexico regaining lost territory in Texas, New Mexico and Arizona. The reaction of the American public persuaded President Woodrow Wilson to bring the United States into the war on the side of the Allied Powers on 6 April 1917.

Military support from the United States was to help turn the tide of war in favour of the Allies.

Death Throes

During the final phase of the war, internal struggles in tsarist Russia, including the revolution of 1917 (see page 62), removed Russia from the conflict by March 1918, ending fighting in the east. This freed German troops on the Eastern Front and shifted the war's focus to the Western Front. With a threat of social revolution spreading across Europe it became increasingly important for European nations to win a quick and decisive victory.

On 21 March 1918, German Quartermaster General Erich Ludendorff launched the 'Spring Offensive', a series of attacks aiming to end the Western Front stalemate and the war. Ludendorff planned to isolate the British then break the French army: 'We should strike at the earliest moment . . . before the Americans can throw strong forces into the scale. We must beat the British.' With 500,000 additional troops brought back from the Russian front, poisonous gas and high explosives, the Germans bombarded the Allies while their elite stormtroopers, hand-picked for fitness and trained to infiltrate enemy rear lines, broke through in thick fog between the French and British armies, advancing 65 kilometres (40 miles). Paris was in reach of German long-range guns but German supply lines became overextended. The Allies co-ordinated their counter-attack ('The Hundred Days', 18 July to 11 November) under French commander Ferdinand Foch, with the welcome reinforcement of American troops.

By midsummer Ludendorff's offensives in Flanders and France had subsided, and by autumn the broken German army had virtually collapsed, with mutiny among sailors and protests among the German population feeling the effects of the blockade.

Socialists were planning a revolution when Kaiser Wilhelm II abdicated on 9 November. The mutiny had convinced German politicians that the Kaiser could no longer rule; the German people blamed him for defeat and for shortages and starvation; and eventually German army leaders withdrew their support for him. The Kaiser went into exile in the neutral Netherlands.

Foch dictated armistice terms to a delegation from the new German socialist government, signed on 11 November 1918 in a railway carriage in the forest of Compiègne, northern France. The armistice ended the fighting but it would take another six months to negotiate peace terms, signed in the Treaty of Versailles on 28 June 1919 (see page 56).

War on an Industrial Scale

Despite the victory of the Allied Powers and the celebrations that followed, the losses and damages to the Allied and Central powers were devastating, with an estimated 40 million military and civilian casualties and 15 million deaths. The war, unprecedented in its impact and fatalities, was the first war of mass armies equipped with weapons to kill on a mass scale, made possible by the technological changes of the Industrial Revolution. Soldiers faced heavy artillery, machine guns, trench mortars, grenades, explosives and toxic gas. Many died from artillery fire, shrapnel wounds and disease contracted in the appalling conditions. Tanks and aircraft were used in combat for the first time, and the first aerial bombing raids on cities by German Zeppelin airships prompted the development of anti-aircraft guns. The first fighter aces arrived, including Germany's 'Red Baron' who shot down eighty enemy aeroplanes, and by 1918 the first bomber aircrafts were attacking targets behind enemy lines. At home, propaganda, spread by mass media, mobilized nations and stimulated a hatred of the opposing side.

The optimism of the nineteenth and early twentieth centuries, including the belief that the rule of law could resolve disputes, had been shattered by the reality of the First World War. As the struggle became more desperate, involving not only armies but whole populations, morality and agreed wartime conventions had been abandoned in a grim fight for survival.

CHAPTER 3

WHEN THE DUST
SETTLES

Europe was deeply scarred by the First World War. Nations competing for territory, industrial power, resources and markets had caused havoc across the continent. Survivors, who had witnessed civilization turn to savagery, hoped the armistice of November 1918 and the Versailles peace treaty of June 1919 would bring lasting peace.

As bankrupt Europe began to rebuild itself, the USA and Japan forged ahead, economically strong from wartime trade. But the American economy, booming during the 'Roaring Twenties', was to crash in 1929, ushering in the Great Depression and years of mass unemployment and social unrest around the world.

Losing faith in democracy and capitalism, some countries turned to totalitarian forms of government. The fascists, originating in Italy, saw liberal democracies as obsolete and opposed the new ideas of socialism and communism. The Italian fascist one-party state led by military dictator Benito Mussolini promoted values of discipline, duty to the nation, and law and order, above liberal values, democracy and individual rights. In Germany, a form of state socialism rejected individual freedoms and promoted economic efficiency to benefit the state: National Socialism, or Nazism.

In the midst of the economic gloom the democratic Weimar Republic of Germany, set up after the First World War, failed under burdens of war reparations, debt and hyperinflation, leaving a door open to the Nazis. Their leader, Adolf Hitler, planned to expand Germany once more. He found a natural ally in Italy's Mussolini and would lead the world into a second global conflict even wider than the first.

Despite the economic and political turmoil of the interwar years, great progress was made in science, including the proposition in 1927 that the universe originated with a 'Big Bang', or explosion, billions of years ago, which created matter out of energy. The theory remains the best explanation for phenomena such as background cosmic microwaves. Much of scientific endeavour during the Second World War would be redirected to developments in weaponry but also to advances in medical treatment.

Bittersweet Homecoming

On the 'eleventh hour of the eleventh day of the eleventh month' of 1918 the guns on the Western Front stopped firing and the Great War ended. In the hushed atmosphere of the battlefield, an Allied corporal reported: 'The Germans came from their trenches, bowed to us and then went away. That was it. There was nothing with which we could celebrate, except cookies.' Celebrations in Paris, London and New York were livelier. The bloody four-year conflict was over.

But many war-weary, malnourished soldiers would never reach home, as a deadly virus spread across battlefields, infecting troops and the wider population. In the two years between 1918 and 1920 the influenza pandemic claimed the lives of an estimated 50 to 100 million – up to 5 per cent of the world's population and several times more than the number killed in the First World War. In neutral Spain its effects were accurately publicized, unlike the politicized war-reporting elsewhere, earning the pandemic its nickname, 'Spanish flu'. The epidemic was the most devastating in modern history.

An American medical journal in 1918 noted that medical science for four and a half years had devoted itself to putting men on the firing line and now must turn to combating 'the greatest enemy of all – infectious disease'. Advances in germ theory, antiseptics and vaccines and the public's acceptance of travel restrictions helped to stop the virus.

Germany Humiliated

At the November 1918 armistice, Germany accepted US President Woodrow Wilson's basis for a just peace: 'Fourteen Points' envisaging a world in which nations resolved their differences through negotiation, not war, without the need for US intervention, and in which people of the same nationality had autonomy to govern themselves. There would be no empire building, a reduction in arms and forces, no secret treaties and an international League of Nations to keep world peace.

With these ideals in mind, the Allied Powers, represented by Woodrow Wilson, the British Prime Minister David Lloyd George and the French Prime Minister Georges

Clemenceau, spent eight months negotiating formal peace terms to present to Germany. These terms were set out in the Treaty of Versailles and signed by the Weimar Republic of Germany (successor to the German Empire) on 28 June 1919 in the Hall of Mirrors, Versailles, near Paris.

The Treaty of Versailles, with other treaties, carved up the territories of the fallen Central Powers: the empires of Germany, Austria-Hungary and the Ottomans. It laid the blame for starting the war squarely on Germany's shoulders and Germany was to pay financial reparations to war-damaged countries. Alsace-Lorraine was given back to France, other German territories were to be administered by Britain, Belgium, Denmark, Czechoslovakia, Poland and Russia as mandates, and the Eastern European states of Estonia, Lithuania and Latvia were created. The German army was reduced to 100,000 men, the navy to six ships and no submarines, and there was to be no German air force. The vital industrial area west of the Rhineland (western Germany) became a demilitarized zone, with an Allied army of occupation for fifteen years. Germany was forbidden to unite again with Austria.

Clemenceau and the French public saw the treaty as just punishment for Germany, but French Marshal Ferdinand Foch considered it too lenient, foreseeing a new generation of Germans seeking revenge for their defeat. 'This is not a peace,' he said, 'it is an armistice for twenty years.' Woodrow Wilson and Lloyd George worried that the treaty was too harsh, seeing an advantage in keeping Germany operational to act as a bulwark against the spread of communism (see page 62).

The German public hated the treaty. A German newspaper, *Deutsche Zeitung*, commented: 'We will never stop until we win back what we deserve.' Economically the treaty was a chain around Germany's neck.

Wilson's ambitious League of Nations became a reality, but the US Congress, fearing loss of US sovereignty and wanting to keep out of European affairs, voted not to join the international initiative, which ultimately was to fail in its objective of maintaining world peace.

House of Habsburg in Ruins

The Habsburgs, rulers of the Holy Roman Empire from the fifteenth to the eighteenth centuries, had governed the Austrian Empire since 1804. In 1867, to balance Europe's rising powers and respond to Hungarian nationalism, the royal family created a dual monarchy with Hungary to govern the Austro-Hungarian Empire. This large multi-ethnic empire had suffered numerous internal conflicts and now it would bear the price of dependency on Germany during the First World War. Ravaged by the war's end, the empire fractured into several independent nation-states. The Czechs had struggled against their Austrian rulers for years, and the Slovaks likewise under Hungary, so it was no surprise when large numbers of Czechs and Slovaks defected on the Russian front during the war and a new state of Czechoslovakia declared independence in 1918.

Likewise, in the southernmost part of the empire, a union of Croats, Serbs and Slovenes proclaimed independence, joined soon after by Serbia to form the Kingdom of Serbs,

Croats and Slovenes. In 1919 it was renamed the Kingdom of Yugoslavia.

The Habsburg monarchy had run its course and on 11 November 1918, the day of the armistice, Charles I, the last ruler of the Austro-Hungarian Empire, dissolved the monarchy and its alliance with Hungary, making Austria a republic. The Allies made separate peace settlements with Austria and Hungary, giving land from both to the new states of Czechoslovakia and Yugoslavia, to the re-established Polish Republic and to the kingdoms of Romania and Italy. Both Austria and Hungary were made to pay reparations to neighbouring war-damaged countries.

The current European Union of states with free movement of goods, capital and labour has been seen as a resurrection of the multinational Austro-Hungarian model and the preceding Holy Roman Empire. Many of the states that surfaced after Austria-Hungary's collapse are now members of the European Union.

Ottoman Break-up

By 1918 the Muslim Ottoman Empire was in tatters. Centred in Anatolia (present-day Turkey), with territory in south-eastern Europe and the Middle East, the multi-ethnic empire had been promised democratic reform by its 'Young Turk' government, after the overthrow of the sultan in 1908, but had delivered only authoritarianism. The empire collapsed shortly before the November 1918 armistice.

The peace treaty of 1920 (Treaty of Sèvres), drawn up by the Allied Powers, shared the Ottoman lands between the Allies, with Greece taking the empire's Aegean coastline.

The Christian Armenians, massacred under the Ottomans, were to have their own state. Ottoman Arab territories, in accordance with a secret (Sykes–Picot) agreement of 1916, would become a mandate ruled by Britain (controlling Iraq, Transjordan and Palestine) and France (controlling Syria and Lebanon) until the people were ready to govern themselves. This was not the immediate independence for which Prince Faisal had launched a desert revolt against his Ottoman masters – with the encouragement of British colonel T. E. Lawrence 'of Arabia' (see page 46). Angered by the treaty terms, the Hashemites and Faisal fought France for Syria's independence, but lost. Prince Faisal, now outcast from Syria, accepted the role of client ruler of Britain's new mandate of Iraq instead.

A further obstacle to Arab independence existed in the Balfour Declaration of 1917. This pledge by British Foreign Secretary Arthur Balfour to the British Jewish community to support the Zionist (Jewish nationalist) aspiration of a Jewish state in the Holy Land (Palestine) would lead to the world's most intractable dispute to date, the Arab–Israeli conflict (see page 149).

The Allies' partition of Ottoman lands disregarded ethnic, sectarian and tribal differences and was to have grave repercussions. Iraq, for example, was formed by merging three Ottoman provinces dominated by Shias, Sunnis and Kurds. The country has since experienced border disputes, war with neighbouring Iran, internal conflicts between Shia and Sunni Muslims, a genocidal campaign against its own rebellious Kurdish population, and an invasion by the United States and its allies. To this day the region remains unstable.

Turkey Rises from the Ashes

The Ottoman government signed the Treaty of Sèvres, but Turks under Gallipoli hero Mustafa Kemal Atatürk (see pages 45–6) rejected it. Atatürk claimed that the Turkish Muslim people needed a homeland in the traditional Turkish territory of Anatolia. His objective was obstructed by Greek claims to western Anatolia and East Thrace, and Britain's occupation of Constantinople (present-day Istanbul), provoking a war of independence between Atatürk's Turkish nationalist forces and Greece in 1919. Atatürk's victory established the modern Turkish republic in 1923, based in Ankara with Atatürk as president.

During the war, Turkey secured north-eastern Anatolia with support from Russia's Bolshevik regime (see page 62). The action was condemned by US President Woodrow Wilson, who had envisioned an independent state there for the Christian Armenians in compensation for their treatment under the Ottomans. But there was no international intervention, prompting Atatürk to comment: 'Poor Wilson did not understand that a frontier which is not defended with bayonets, force and honour cannot be secured by any other principle.'

The incident demonstrated the weakness of the League of Nations. Turkish borders were finally agreed in the Treaty of Lausanne of 1923. Armenia was annexed by Russia's Bolsheviks and became part of the Soviet Union in 1922.

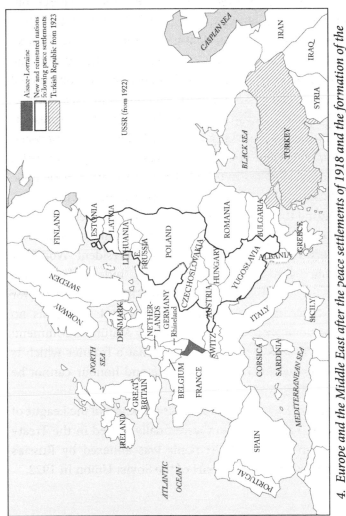

4. *Europe and the Middle East after the peace settlements of 1918 and the formation of the Turkish Republic in 1923.*

Radical Russia

In February 1917 a lethal fusion of war losses, privation at home and lack of government structures to integrate the working classes exploded into revolution in Russia. Tsar Nicholas II, whose concessions towards reform following Russia's first revolution in 1905 had never materialized (see page 27), was blamed for Russia's misery and toppled from power. In his place, a provisional government of 'revolutionary democracy' continued to fight in the global conflict. But more radical revolutionary ideas were spreading, leading to a third revolution in October 1917, this time by communist Bolsheviks, who overthrew the Provisional Government in Petrograd (St Petersburg, renamed Petrograd in 1914 under the Imperial government, Leningrad by the Bolsheviks in 1924 and St Petersburg once more in 1991 when the Soviet Union collapsed).

Members of the Bolshevik Party, a revolutionary wing of the Russian Social Democratic Labour Party, saw themselves as the vanguard of the working classes, promising food, land, control of factories and a voice in law-making to the workers. The party ruthlessly used the 'Cheka' secret police to eliminate class enemies. Its leader, Vladimir Lenin, exiled by tsarists for revolutionary activities, returned to Petrograd in 1917 aided by Germany, which saw him as a destabilizing force in Russia. As predicted, Lenin removed Russia's will to fight the First World War and four months after the revolution his government negotiated peace with Germany at Brest-Litovsk (now in Belarus) in March 1918.

The Bolsheviks took power over former territories of the Russian Empire, leading to a drawn-out civil war.

During the catastrophe, the Bolsheviks killed the Russian tsar and his family to prevent their rescue by the White Army, a confederation of anti-communist forces fighting the Bolsheviks' Red Army. Despite foreign intervention including US troops, the Red Army was victorious and established the Union of Soviet Socialist Republics (Soviet Union, or USSR) in 1922, a one-party federal state governed by the Russian Communist Party based in Moscow. The civil war had claimed up to 12 million casualties.

The political ideas of the Soviet Union were based on those of Lenin and nineteenth-century economist Karl Marx. The Bolsheviks sought a transition from capitalism to a socialist state ruled by the working-class majority, 'a dictatorship of the proletariat'. They would focus on establishing socialism in the USSR and support

5. *Soviet Russia, Transcaucasia, Ukraine and Byelorussia (Belarus) unite to form the USSR in 1922.*

communist revolutions elsewhere. Their ultimate goal was 'pure communism', a classless and stateless society characterized by common ownership of the means of production and distribution. In reality, the Bolshevik socialist state became organized by strict adherence to decisions of the Communist Party, a dictatorship that claimed to represent working-class interests.

Reports of the new state and society in Russia inspired workers around the world and filled Western governments (particularly the US) with fear. Although Russia had fought as one of the Allies in the First World War, the Allies refused to recognize the Bolshevik government and did not invite Russia to the peace talks at Versailles.

Iron Fist of Stalin

Lenin died in 1924. In his quest for power, the General Secretary of the Russian Communist Party, Joseph Stalin, used political manipulation to discredit his rival, Leon Trotsky, the leader of the Red Army, who went into exile and was later assassinated by a Soviet agent.

In sole charge by 1928, Stalin began the first of several 'Five Year' economic plans to boost Soviet industry, introducing targets for factory workers and establishing collective farms by taking land from kulaks (land-owning peasants). The failure of the latter caused widespread famine in the Ukraine during the 1930s. Stalin ruled as a dictator of the Soviet Union until his death in 1953, destroying political enemies and deporting millions to labour camps.

Although Stalin's policies developed industry and built a military strength that would rival the USA in the Cold

War (see page 155), his repressive government failed to grant people their fundamental civil rights. The appeal of Russian communism gradually waned in the second half of the twentieth century. Life under a single-party totalitarian regime such as Stalin's inspired English author George Orwell to write his dystopian novel, *Nineteen Eighty-Four*, published after the war in 1949.

China the Republic

China had started the twentieth century in turmoil. The unpopular Qing imperial dynasty was decadent and corrupt, its once proud officialdom was incompetent, and the country did not know how to handle relations with Europeans or with its resurgent Japanese neighbour. The humiliation of the Boxer Rebellion in 1899–1901 (see pages 18–9) fuelled the growth of nationalism.

The nationalists were epitomized in Chinese revolutionary Sun Yat-sen, who thought that the decaying Chinese imperial line should give way to democracy and that China needed to modernize and industrialize to match the West.

Sun influenced the revolution that toppled the Qing dynasty in 1911–12 and became the first president of the Republic of China in 1912, ending 4,000 years of imperial rule. He then led the Chinese Nationalist Party (the Kuomintang or KMT) against warlords who controlled much of China in a turbulent era of war and instability.

May Fourth Movement

When China joined the Allies in the First World War in 1917, sending more than 100,000 troops to fight for the Allied side, it was on the understanding that Chinese territory surrendered to Germany, such as the east coastal province of Shandong, would be returned to China at the end of the war. Chinese intellectuals stirred by the ideas of US President Woodrow Wilson had high hopes in the Treaty of Versailles (see page 56). But these were dashed when the outcome was a transfer of Shandong territories to China's rival, Japan.

The failure of the Chinese delegation to influence the Versailles Treaty sparked a revolt on 4 May 1919, when more than 3,000 students demonstrated in Peking (Beijing). Protests supported by intellectuals, patriotic merchants and workers spread across Chinese cities, sparking a New Culture Movement, an upsurge in Chinese nationalism and a boycott of Japanese products. Historian Theodore H. Von Laue called it 'the first stirring of patriotic mass politics in China'. It marked a turning point that would lead China towards communism.

China Goes Red

Disappointed by the West's treatment of China, Sun Yat-sen turned to the Bolshevik communists, who helped his nationalist KMT government establish an army and greater political control. The Soviets encouraged an alliance between the KMT and the then small Chinese Communist Party in 1923, in order to fight the Chinese warlords.

Sun died in 1925. His successor, Chiang Kai-shek, led a military and political offensive to unify the country and defeat the warlords (the Northern Expedition), and by 1927 had successfully extended KMT influence. At this point, Chiang, a ruthless military commander, unexpectedly turned against his communist allies, his forces massacring communist activists in Shanghai. The survivors fled to remote areas in southern China and Chiang declared the KMT the official government of the unified state, but he had sparked a civil war between his nationalists and the Communist Party of China.

Chiang's tough approach posed a threat to Japan's militaristic and expansionist ambitions and in 1931 Japan invaded the important Chinese province of Manchuria on a false pretext, installing a puppet ruler, Puyi, the heir to the old Chinese imperial family. While Japan bullied China and strove for control of the region, Chiang continued his campaign against Chinese communists. In 1934, to escape capture by Chiang's forces, Mao Zedong (then known as Mao Tse-Tung; the future Chairman of the People's Republic of China) led communist forces on a Long March of 12,500 kilometres (8,000 miles) between the southern Jiangxi province and the remote north-western Shaanxi province. The march was a heroic achievement and Mao Zedong became a leading figure of Chinese communism.

A full-scale Japanese invasion in 1937 forced the KMT and the Chinese communists to collaborate temporarily, fighting a united front in the second Sino-Japanese War.

Ahead of advancing Japanese troops, Chiang's government abandoned Shanghai, and in December 1937 Japanese violence against women and prisoners of war in the KMT capital, Nanjing, shocked the world (the 'Rape of Nanjing'). Japan's continued onslaught would propel China into the Second World War on the side of the Allies when the USA declared war on Japan in December 1941.

Following the Second World War and Japan's surrender in 1945, the KMT and Communists would continue their civil war. Despite aid from the USA, the KMT nationalists were eventually defeated by the Communists in 1949 and fled to the island of Taiwan. Mao Zedong made a victorious entry into Beijing, announcing that the new Chinese government would be 'under the leadership of the Communist Party of China'.

Seeds of a Superpower

While European countries struggled to rebuild broken economies and infrastructure after the First World War, the USA enjoyed an economic boom fed by repayments of war loans with interest by Allied countries and profits from America's industry. America of the 1920s showed the economic potential that would make it the world's principal superpower by the end of the century.

Expansion of America's munitions industries from wartime orders spread to electrical goods, chemicals, automobiles and related industries, aided by high import tariffs limiting foreign competition (policies of the Harding and Coolidge presidencies, 1921–9). Customers and markets neglected by European countries were taken over and US companies developed the ability to raise finance by selling shares on the Stock Exchange.

Industrial expansion coincided with a consumer boom stimulated by hire-purchase arrangements, allowing people to borrow money to purchase cars, telephones, radios and labour-saving electrical household goods. Wartime skills in propaganda transferred to advertising. A record number of cars purchased in the USA in the 1920s increased the demand for decent roads, and more of them (the USA had few roads prior to the twentieth century), leading to a huge drive for road construction, which was often privately funded.

Jazz music and the Charleston dance became popular in the carefree 'Roaring Twenties'; the Jazz Age was the subject of F. Scott Fitzgerald's bestselling novel *The Great Gatsby*, published in 1925. By 1924 American jazz music and culture was spreading to Europe, where living standards were improving with social housing schemes for the working classes and a small but growing percentage of housing equipped with electrical power, indoor plumbing and sewage systems. Public health was also improving due to the discovery of disease-preventing nutrients in the first decades of the century, including vitamins. Women liberated from the corseted silhouette wore skirts shortened to just below the knee and dresses in the 'garçonne' style, based on designs by French fashion designer Coco Chanel. Rebellious young women with bobbed hair became known as flappers.

In 1928 the new Republican president Herbert Hoover declared a 'triumph over poverty'. But in spite of his confidence the economy was in trouble: hardships were continuing for farmers and African-Americans isolated from the benefits of the boom years, women were poorly paid in an unequal society and America was teetering on the edge of a stock-market crash that would plunge the world into economic misery.

Wall Street Crash

On 29 October 1929 the financial bubble burst in New York, precipitating a global crisis of capitalism. The ill-regulated market saw share prices tumble, causing panic selling on Wall Street of more than 16 million shares in one day. Banks closed, bankrupting private businesses and wiping out investors. America's war loans to Great Britain and France were recalled and protectionist customs barriers blocked imports of foreign goods, spreading the effects of the crisis around the world.

It was the beginning of the Great Depression, a period of mass unemployment that affected most industrialized nations. Between 1929 and 1933 world trade shrank by 65 per cent in dollar value. In New York angry unemployed workers marched in the streets offering to work for a dollar a week. Dust storms in America's Great Plains during 1934 brought further woe and led thousands of Oklahoma farmers to travel westwards, a chaotic migration described by John Steinbeck in *The Grapes of Wrath*.

US President Hoover, widely blamed for the crisis, was replaced by the Democrat candidate Franklin D. Roosevelt in 1932, who promised a 'new deal for the American people', involving reforms, public works and an end to the unpopular 'Prohibition', or ban on alcohol. The Depression lasted until the late 1930s, when the Second World War stimulated industry and created jobs.

Democracy on a Roller-coaster

Following the disaster of the First World War, US President Woodrow Wilson encouraged nations across war-torn Europe to adopt the wider political base of multi-party democratic government, giving people a say in the decisions of government. The Republic of Turkey, emerging from the ashes of the Ottoman Empire, was born with a parliamentary constitution (see page 60), and new or revived states from the imperial ruins of Austria-Hungary, Germany and the border areas of Russia adopted systems of representative parliamentary democracy, including Czechoslovakia, Yugoslavia, Poland, Austria, Hungary, Finland, Estonia, Latvia and Lithuania. The southern part of Ireland, independent from Britain from 1922 following a bitter war, created its own democratic republic, the Irish Free State. But despite the spread of democracy, governments faced major problems in countries where the ideals of democracy competed with violence, repression, manipulation by powerful elites and destabilization by war and economic failure.

The more successful democracies around the world widened their franchise (see page 116). Women had earned respect in wartime roles and women's suffrage, a militant issue earlier in the century, was now an acceptable proposition in most Western nations. The working class, who had fought bravely for their countries, demanded the same rights as wealthier people. Public pressure to give everyone the vote led to universal suffrage in Germany, the Netherlands and Poland in 1919, Britain in 1928, Turkey in 1934, France in 1944 and Italy by 1945. In the USA women could vote from 1920; however, many African-Americans, while constitutionally enfranchised in 1870, in practice were unable to vote until 1965 because of various restrictions.

The Ugly Face of Fascism

In 1920s Italy, democracy collapsed, replaced by an extreme right-wing political ideology known as fascism. The fascists were nationalists who rejected communism and espoused complete subservience to the state (totalitarianism): militaristic and elitist rule at the expense of democracy and liberalism.

Italy's small territorial gains offered in the Treaty of Versailles (see page 56) were seen as poor reward for a costly war. Economic instability led to social crisis (the Biennio Rosso, or 'Two Red Years', 1919–20) from which emerged the fascists, who promised to stem the spread of communism and bring glory to Italy. The group was founded by the charismatic Benito Mussolini supported by the Blackshirts, his violent militia. Mussolini glorified armed struggle – in 1932 he wrote: 'Only war brings all human energies to a maximum tension and imprints the mark of nobility upon the peoples who have the virtue to face it'; he rejected the 'sickly internationalism' of Lenin and Woodrow Wilson. From 1925 Mussolini, promoted as the nation's saviour, led the one-party totalitarian state whose expansionist foreign policy resulted in the invasion of Ethiopia in 1935. Italy and Germany, on opposing sides during the First World War, developed a bond in their fight against communism and socialism, which was formalized in the 1939 'Pact of Steel', committing both countries to mutual support in the event of war.

The reaction to the spread of socialism reached Spain in the 1930s, a country badly affected by the Great Depression (see page 70). Neutral during the First World War, Spain had become a republic after King Alfonso XIII fled in 1931 on the election of an anti-monarchist left-wing government. The ensuing political struggle climaxed in a military coup by right-wing nationalists in 1936, led by General Francisco Franco, which grew into a civil war across the politically divided country. Franco and the nationalists were supported by Nazi Germany and fascist Italy, along with monarchists, the Roman Catholic Church, the army and landowners. The nationalists felt they were defending Spanish traditions from a socialist-leaning government that had begun to take land from aristocrats, was moving education from the Catholic Church towards secular institutions and was reducing the army's strength.

On the other side were republicans ('Loyalists'), loyal to the left-leaning republic, supported by communist Russia and socialist Mexico, with unofficial aid from France, which feared being surrounded by fascist powers (Germany and Italy) if Spain fell to the nationalists. Idealists, socialists and communists from all over the world were drawn to fight against fascism. The Republicans felt they were defending an elected government. British author George Orwell wrote in 1943 about his experiences with the Republicans: 'Here we are, soldiers of a revolutionary army, defending Democracy against Fascism, fighting a war which is *about* something'. The better-equipped nationalists won and Franco was to rule Spain from 1939 for thirty-six years.

Franco's dictatorship ruthlessly suppressed all opposition but his political regime ended with his death in 1975. With the support of Franco's chosen successor, King Juan Carlos I, the country made the transition to democracy and a constitutional monarchy. Statues and memorials to Franco were removed and today Spain condemns the murders and human rights violations that took place during his reign.

Weimar Republic in Crisis

Germany at the end of the First World War reeled from the shock of defeat. Its population on the brink of starvation was rebellious and the country's economy was in ruins. A sailors' revolt in Kiev sparked Germany's 'November Revolution' (November 1918 to August 1919), a bloodless mutiny that led to the abdication of the Kaiser and a new democratic government.

The democratic Republic of Germany had the difficult task of rebuilding the damaged nation. A need for reform was recognized by the leading party in Germany's Reichstag (parliament), the Social Democrat Party, but how much change was needed? Radical socialists, including activist

Rosa Luxemburg, wanted a 'dictatorship of the proletariat' – though not on Russia's one-party Bolshevik model (see page 63). Luxemburg and her group of revolutionaries (the Spartacists) founded the German Communist Party in December 1918, leading to clashes in Berlin between Spartacists and Freikorps, the right-wing nationalists and battle-hardened returning soldiers who hated communists and left-wing politics. In the chaos, the government abandoned the capital city and set up parliament in Weimar (from which the German republic derived its name from 1919 to 1933). Spartacists were arrested and Luxemburg and other leaders, left to the mercy of the Freikorps, were murdered.

The Weimar government was heavily criticized when it signed the Treaty of Versailles in June 1919 (see page 56). Right-wing journalist Wolfgang Kapp, backed by the army and the Freikorps, seized the opportunity to occupy Berlin in March 1920 (the Kapp Putsch), with plans to establish a right-wing nationalist government. The democratic government was saved when 12 million workers joined a mass strike, paralysing the country.

In 1923 Weimar Germany faced bankruptcy and defaulted on its reparation payments, leading to occupation of Germany's industrial Ruhr valley by French and Belgian troops. This further stifled the German economy, contributing to hyperinflation that destroyed the German currency, the mark, and the savings of middle-class Germans. A loaf of bread costing 250 marks at the beginning of the year had risen to 200,000 million marks by November. Germans were forced to collect their wages in suitcases and paper money became so worthless it was used as kindling.

Hardships caused by hyperinflation led to political polarization and revolts, which were swiftly dealt with by the army. The extreme right in Bavaria, supported by paramilitaries and led by ex-soldier Adolf Hitler, planned to march on Berlin and proclaim a national dictatorship, as Mussolini had done with the fascists in Italy in 1922. But when Hitler failed to win the backing of the German army he made do with a small revolt in a Munich beer hall on 8 November 1923 (the Beer Hall Putsch), which collapsed under police gunfire. Hitler was imprisoned and the crisis subsided.

Germany's currency stabilized and the 'Roaring Twenties', from 1924 to 1929, were economically productive. Parliamentary democracy and the Republic had survived, but the 1929 Wall Street Crash in New York was round the corner (see page 70).

Rise of Nazism

As the Great Depression of 1929 plunged Germany into a new economic crisis Adolf Hitler was poised to rise. After the Beer Hall Putsch in Munich in 1923, Hitler had been sentenced to five years in prison, though he served less than nine months. While incarcerated he wrote his political memoir, *Mein Kampf* (published 1925–6), expressing his antipathy towards the Jews and communism. During the early years of the Weimar Republic, Hitler became a key member of the National Socialist German Workers' (Nazi) Party. With the support of Nazi paramilitaries, the

Stormtroopers (SA), he spread a campaign of fear against communism. The SA wore brown uniforms, modelled on Mussolini's fascist Blackshirts in Italy, and were drawn from the Freikorps and other violent groups who supported the Nazis.

The Nazis gained popularity and in January 1933, with the help of his propaganda chief Joseph Goebbels, Hitler became German Chancellor, heading a coalition government. A month later the Reichstag was destroyed by fire. Hitler blamed the communists and used the fire as a pretext to assume emergency powers. He abolished the Reichstag, and democratic government, hated by Hitler, ceased in Germany. In March the same year the Nazi police sent communists, socialists and trade unionists to the first Nazi concentration camp at Dachau, where they were used as slave labour.

Reparation payments had shackled Germany's economy since the Treaty of Versailles and Hitler had long considered the treaty a humiliation. In 1933 he dramatically increased his following by suspending future repayments. Tightening the Nazis' grip, he encouraged supporters to burn 'un-German' cultural items, including books by Jewish and left-wing authors. Political opponents were murdered, including SA leaders in 1934 – a ploy to get the German army on Hitler's side (the 'Night of the Long Knives').

When German President Paul von Hindenburg died in 1934, Hitler proclaimed himself Führer (leader) of the Third Reich or Third Empire, as Nazi Germany called itself. (The first empire was the medieval Holy Roman Empire, and the second was the German Empire of 1871–1918.)

In the years up to 1939, many Germans saw Hitler's dictatorship as bringing positive economic change. Hitler used propaganda to develop an image of himself as the saviour of Germany, provoking fanatical support in the elimination of all enemies of the Reich.

The Nazis' loyal paramilitary security force, the black-uniformed SS (Schutzstaffel, or 'Protective Squadron'), brutally carried out Hitler's wishes. Headed by extreme racist Heinrich Himmler, the ranks of these political soldiers swelled and took control of Germany's police forces. Waffen-SS members were recruited as special military units and the General SS controlled police and 'racial' matters. By 1939 a quarter of a million SS had been schooled in racial hatred and loyalty to the Führer.

As Germany rearmed in open violation of the Treaty of Versailles, Hitler reassured the world that the military build-up was solely for defence. Berlin hosted the Olympic Games in 1936 but in the background Hitler was busy solidifying secret plans to expand Germany and extend his war. 'Germany needs more space for the preservation and growth of the German people,' he told his top generals. Hitler's other major goal was a final reckoning with the Jews.

CHAPTER 4

TOTAL WAR

The Second World War involved sixty-one countries and about three-quarters of the global population. It demanded the full resources of the major participants' economies and industries, along with the efforts of every sector of the countries' populations. The timely discovery of antibiotics by Scottish bacteriologist Alexander Fleming in 1928 helped to save the lives of many soldiers wounded and at risk of infection, but still the casualties of this war were unprecedented: an estimated 25 million soldiers, sailors and airmen were killed, and even more civilians – between 30 and 60 million – lost their lives. In addition the Second Sino-Japanese War, a conflict that became part of the global war, caused the deaths of between 10 and 25 million Chinese civilians and over 4 million Chinese and Japanese military personnel.

After hostilities ended there was a new geopolitical map: communism dominated Eastern Europe, the USA became a superpower, while Western Europe's influence in global affairs diminished.

Setting the Stage for War

In 1936 Hitler embarked on his first act of German expansion, taking control of the industrial Rhineland in western Germany, which had been under Allied occupation since the end of the First World War. Two years later, in contravention of the Treaty of Versailles (see page 56), came the Anschluss, unifying Germany with German-speaking Austria, Hitler's native homeland. The League of Nations founded at the end of the First World War proved ineffective at stopping Germany, while the Allies, Britain and France, hoped through a policy of appeasement to prevent another major war. Again ignoring conditions imposed by the Treaty of Versailles, Germany had rearmed, building up its army and investing in modern tanks and aircraft. This triggered a temporary boom in the global economy as Britain, the USA and the USSR tried to match Germany's potential threat by boosting their own military capabilities.

Hitler wanted all German-speaking nations in Europe to be part of Germany and made it clear that he intended to take over the Sudetenland, the German-speaking part of Czechoslovakia. In September 1938 Britain and France signed the Munich Agreement with Germany, allowing Hitler to annex that territory on the understanding that he would make no more expansionist demands. Neville Chamberlain, the British prime minister, announced that the agreement gave 'peace for our time', but just a few months later Hitler was demanding the Baltic free port of Danzig (now Gdansk) and a part of Poland, whose government refused to cede any territory.

The Alliances Take Shape

Germany and Italy first formed an alliance in 1936: the Rome–Berlin Axis. It was reinforced by their Pact of Steel in May 1939. Then in August Germany formed the unexpected Non-Aggression Pact with the Soviet Union, as Hitler and the Russian leader Stalin plotted to divide Poland between them. In September 1940 Japan joined the Axis Alliance after signing the Tripartite Pact with Germany and Italy.

France and Poland had been allies since 1921, and during 1939 Britain also agreed to support Poland with a formal military alliance. So when Germany invaded Poland on 1 September 1939, Britain declared war on Germany.

Blitzkrieg

Hitler had prepared well. The German army on the eve of war was 2.5 million strong, with five panzer (tank) divisions, and the air force (Luftwaffe) had more than 1,000 fighter planes and bombers. When the Soviet Red Army invaded Poland from the east, the unequal struggle became hopeless and Poland fell on 6 October. This was to be the pattern for German advances in the first part of the war. The well-oiled German war machine, using modern mechanized equipment and covered from the air by the Luftwaffe, employed its tactic of Blitzkrieg ('Lightning War') to steamroller through Belgium, the Netherlands, Luxembourg, Denmark and Norway. None offered any military match for the Third Reich: the Dutch army did not have any tanks at all.

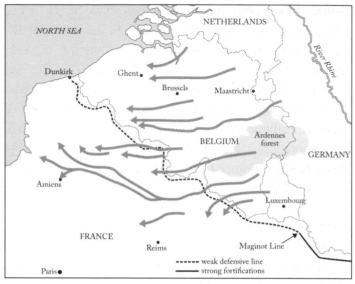

6. *The German advance through Belgium to France.*

France Falls

In contrast to Blitzkrieg, France kept its large and well-equipped army behind the Maginot Line, a complex of defensive fortifications that ran from the Alps to the Belgium border near Luxembourg.

Conscription in Britain had begun before war broke out, so a British Expeditionary Force (BEF) stood with French and Belgian armies to face the Germans in early May 1940 as the Nazis forged their way to France. Then came the first flaw in the Allies' battle plan: the Maginot Line proved no barrier at all, as the German panzer tanks pushed through the Ardennes forest, left practically undefended since France had thought it was impenetrable.

Followed by mobile infantry, the panzers split the Allied forces, trapping some on the coast. With Italy entering the war on the German side in June 1940, it took just six weeks for the Nazi conquest of France to be complete. The Free French resistance movement rallied under General Charles de Gaulle leading France's defence from Britain, while Marshal Philippe Pétain, France's hero of Verdun, formed a collaborationist French government under the Nazis in Vichy to spare France from a repeat of the horrors of the First World War.

The Secret War

Members of the French Resistance and other partisan movements came from all walks of life. Among them was philosopher Jean-Paul Sartre who, with his partner Simone de Beauvoir, would go on to explore existentialism. Many resistance leaders were to play a part in postwar politics, for example Josip Tito, who became dictator of Yugoslavia.

It was a dangerous life for spies and partisans: the German SS (the elite corps of the Nazi party) usually executed those they captured and carried out savage acts of reprisal. After senior SS official Reinhard Heydrich was assassinated in Czechoslovakia in 1942, the SS murdered more than 200 people from the village of Lidice.

The armed partisans fought a guerrilla war against the Germans across occupied Europe. Common forms of resistance included assassinations, sabotage and uprisings, such as those in the Warsaw Ghetto, Poland, in 1943 and 1944. In August 1944 the French Resistance were to rise up against the German occupation of Paris, contributing to the liberation of the city later that month. Passive resistance included the political protests in Bulgaria that prevented deportation of the country's Jewish population, and covert go-slows on train networks that hindered the movement of German forces after the Allied invasion to liberate Europe in 1944. Simply by hiding radios, passing on messages, or reporting on German troop movements, thousands of ordinary people in occupied countries helped the resistance movement.

Spies and secret agents parachuted behind enemy lines to supply resistance movements or to gain vital information. Some of their equipment was as fantastical as that found in a James Bond story, such as bombs to be placed in dead rats.

The Dunkirk Evacuation

Hitler's tanks and mobile infantry had proven unstoppable, and in late May 1940 the British Expeditionary Force (BEF) was trapped at Dunkirk, on the northern coast of France. But instead of sending his armies onwards, Hitler held them back, ordering the Luftwaffe to bomb the Allied troops on the ground. This short breathing space allowed the Royal Air Force to arrive and defend the ground forces, and gave time for Britain to appeal for help from civilians.

Sailors ranging from teenagers to grandfathers, manning a flotilla of 'little ships' (fishing boats, lifeboats and yachts) crossed the English Channel repeatedly, bringing British, French and Belgian soldiers off the Dunkirk beaches. It was a triumph in defeat: most (but not all) of the BEF was rescued, even though the bulk of their equipment was left behind. Then Britain, with its empire, stood alone against the Nazis.

The Battle of Britain

On 10 May 1940 Winston Churchill became British prime minister after Chamberlain resigned. Churchill led the country in its darkest days as that July the Battle of Britain began in the skies. At first the Luftwaffe only bombed military sites. Then, in September, the Blitz started, with nightly raids on London and other cities. Hermann Göring, commander of the Luftwaffe, had claimed that his planes would clear the way for a German invasion of Britain, but he was wrong. Though greatly outnumbered, Britain's Royal Air Force (RAF) and its allies eventually made the Luftwaffe attacks too costly for Germany to maintain with such intensity, and in October Hitler abandoned plans to invade. The RAF's defence of Britain was one of the key moments in the war. Churchill commemorated the RAF with his famous speech 'Never was so much owed by so many to so few . . .'

Air raids continued throughout the war, although in 1941 the Luftwaffe's focus turned to the battlefields that had opened up in the USSR. For Britain, with no troops in Europe, bombing was the only way to damage the enemy's military or industrial targets, but conventional bombing raids were inaccurate and dangerous: few targets were hit and RAF losses were high. Proposed by Air Marshal Sir Arthur 'Bomber' Harris, a new pattern of aerial warfare developed: area bombing, known today as carpet-bombing.

Harris's test raid in spring 1942 involved more than 1,000 planes and destroyed 2.4 square kilometres (600 acres) of the industrial city of Cologne, with only thirty-nine planes lost to enemy fighter planes or flak (anti-aircraft fire from the ground).

Sinking and Scuttling

Long before British and German soldiers met on the battlefield, their seamen were doing their worst in the Battle of the Atlantic. On 3 September 1939, two days after the invasion of Poland, a German U-boat sank the British liner *Athenia*, killing 117 passengers and crew. From then on, British ships travelled in defended convoys.

Germany achieved a sensational success in October 1939 when U-boat *U-47* entered the British naval base at Scapa Flow and torpedoed the battleship *Royal Oak*, killing 833 men. The Royal Navy retaliated in December, badly damaging the Atlantic raider *Graf Spee*, which limped into harbour in Montevideo, Uruguay, to be scuttled by her captain rather than let her fall into the hands of the Allies. Parts of the wreck can still be seen beside the harbour.

Both sides laid coastal mines to try to impose blockades, and the big guns of the navies, the battleships, played cat and mouse with each other over the seas. Overall, the Allies lost many millions of tons of shipping to U-boats. In September 1940 the Royal Navy was reinforced when the USA transferred fifty destroyers to Britain in return for leasing military bases on British possessions around the world. The following year a formal Lend-Lease Agreement was signed between the USA and the UK, allowing American planes, tanks and guns to be lent or leased to the Allies. US President Franklin D. Roosevelt referred to America as the 'arsenal of democracy'.

U-boats hunted in 'wolf packs' using messages coded on Enigma machines to relay information about the position and strength of Allied shipping, as well as orders for attack. They had a devastating impact until one of their Enigma machines was captured in 1941 and Allied code-breakers at Bletchley Park in Buckinghamshire began to decipher their messages. Finally the Allies' Atlantic convoys had the edge, avoiding U-boats while the navy hunted them down. By May 1943 the Allies achieved supremacy of the Atlantic. After Germany invaded the USSR, the naval struggle concentrated in the Arctic, as the Allies attempted to supply the Soviet Union with arms.

Nazi Advance Freezes Solid

Having been stopped at the English Channel by the RAF, Hitler turned to the Balkans and further east. Countries such as Bulgaria joined the Axis alliance of Germany, Italy and Japan, while other countries, such as Greece and Yugoslavia, were conquered. Then in Operation Barbarossa in June 1941, Hitler turned on his old ally, sending 4 million troops into the Stalin-led Soviet Union, the largest invasion force in history. He had several motivations. Communism was a natural enemy of Nazism and the Non-Intervention Pact between Germany and the USSR was always a temporary expedient. Hitler's philosophy held that Russians (Slavs) were an inferior people; in Nazi-occupied areas of the USSR Russians were starved to death, making room for more Aryans. And, of course, Germany was desperate for Russian natural resources.

At first Blitzkrieg worked: the Germans charged forward in pincer movements cutting off huge pockets of Soviet troops. By early December the Germans had taken the cities of Kiev and Kharkov, were besieging Leningrad and were just 30 kilometres (19 miles) from Moscow when the Russian winter froze their advance. Better prepared for the weather, the Russian Red Army rallied and began successful counter-attacks, pushing the Axis forces away from Moscow. Hitler, however, would not consider the tactical withdrawal his advisers recommended.

The Battle of Stalingrad

In June 1942 Hitler launched two new offensives, towards the Caucasus region and the important industrial city of Stalingrad (now Volgograd). The battle for the city took place from street to street, building to building, as desperate defenders were pushed into a narrow strip beside the Volga River. But the German lines were overstretched and their army suffered serious losses.

Then the Red Army took Hitler by surprise by launching a two-pronged attack from the surrounding countryside, bursting through the weak German flanks and encircling the

Nazi forces in Stalingrad. After two months in freezing near-starvation conditions, the Germans disobeyed orders and surrendered.

Nearly 2 million soldiers died, were captured or went missing in the Battle of Stalingrad; casualties among Russian civilians were estimated at 40,000. Hitler saw it as a major humiliation, but more importantly, the Soviet victory put a stop to the Nazi advance. The battle was a clear turning point in the war: the moment the tide turned in favour of the Allies. From then on the Red Army advanced and the Nazis retreated. On 5 July 1943 the two forces fought the largest tank battle in history at Kursk, and once again the Soviets were victorious. They did not stop until they entered Berlin nearly a year later.

Hunting the Desert Fox

When the war began, Britain controlled the strategic sea passages from the Mediterranean: Gibraltar at the western end and the Suez Canal in the east. Italy had territorial ambitions in Africa and in late 1940 attacked Egypt from its colony in Libya. The Italian attack was a disaster and by early 1941 almost all of Italy's African territories were taken by Britain, together with 130,000 prisoners of war. On 5 May 1941 Ethiopian Emperor Haile Selassie, who had been in exile since the Italian conquest of his country in 1936, returned to Ethiopia.

Once Germany had completed its conquest of the Balkans and Greece it came to Italy's aid. Germany's Afrika

Korps under Field Marshal Erwin Rommel, the 'Desert Fox', arrived in North Africa in February 1941 and pushed the Allies out of Libya. A series of battles fought with tanks and armoured cars then saw both sides first advance, then retreat along the Western Desert. The port city of Tobruk in Libya changed hands several times during the war. Australian and New Zealand units had fought in the North African campaign since its beginning, and those besieged by Rommel in Tobruk in 1941 proudly took the nickname 'Rats of Tobruk' originally given to them in derision by Nazi propandist Lord Haw-Haw.

Rommel launched a new offensive in June 1942 that was only stopped at the First Battle of El Alamein, not far from Alexandria in Egypt. At this point, there was a very real danger that he might go on to seize the Suez Canal and its access to Middle Eastern oil supplies that were vital to Britain's war effort.

In August 1942 a new Allied commander arrived in the region: General Bernard Montgomery. Under his direction, in October the Allies mustered a devastating attack and at the Second Battle of El Alamein routed Rommel's tanks, spending the following four months chasing the Axis forces back across North Africa, through Libya and behind the fortified Mareth Line in Tunisia. It was the deciding moment of the Desert War.

The final stage of the North African campaign began in November 1942 with Operation Torch, an attempt to create a pincer around the German and Italian forces. American and British soldiers landed in Morocco and Algeria, countries controlled by Vichy France, with General George

S. Patten leading the Americans to capture the strategic port of Casablanca. While the collaborationist Vichy French in Morocco opposed the invasion, in Algeria the French Resistance rose up and took control.

The Allies' plan worked and in May 1943 the Axis army in Tunisia surrendered. The latter part of the Desert War contributed greatly to the overall Allied strategy. It took some of the pressure off the USSR, captured hundreds of thousands of experienced Axis troops, and gave the Allies a springboard for the invasion of Italy. This began in July 1943 with an assault on Sicily that overran the island but failed to prevent Axis forces escaping to mainland Italy.

On 24 July 1943 the Italian government switched sides and ousted Mussolini, agreeing an armistice with the Allies on 3 September. In the chaos that followed, German forces rescued Mussolini and tried to fill the gaps in the Italian defences; the Allies gave chase up the length of Italy before stumbling to a halt in the mountainous north. Not until 2 May 1945 did the Axis forces in Italy surrender.

The Red Sun Rises

The Japanese Empire had signalled its arrival on the world stage by defeating Russia in 1905 (see page 26), then colonizing Korea in 1910 as part of its plan to extend political and military influence across Asia.

Participation in the First World War had boosted Japan's economic growth, but the global depression in the late 1920s, as in Italy and Germany, had given rise to an extreme nationalism. Western influences in Japan were rejected in favour of traditional Japanese samurai warrior values:

courage, obedience and strict discipline. Surrender was unthinkable, and a soldier who allowed himself to be taken prisoner was deemed to have lost all honour.

In 1931 Japan took Manchuria in north-east China, then in 1937 launched the Second Sino-Japanese War, a full-scale invasion of China. The well-trained Japanese army captured the cities of Shanghai and Beijing, before seizing the then capital Nanjing and embarking on an orgy of rape and murder – the 'Rape of Nanjing'. However, Japan would never consolidate its grip on China.

Wary of Japanese expansion, the USA had built up its forces in the Pacific as a potential counterweight, creating a strong naval presence at Pearl Harbor, Hawaii. A selective military draft was introduced in America in 1940 and, even though the USA was a non-combatant, American volunteers fought with the Allies from the beginning of the war.

Japan eyed the rich resources of European Pacific colonies and began to move troops into Vichy France's territories in Indochina, creating a springboard towards Burma, Malaya and Singapore, Britain's centre of power in the Far East. But with Britain engaged in Europe, America was Japan's greatest threat in the Pacific.

Surprise Attack on Pearl Harbor

Japan believed that the USA would not stomach a lengthy campaign, so even while negotiating a peace treaty it sent submarines and aircraft carriers towards Pearl Harbor. The attack on the base in the early morning of 7 December 1941 was a complete surprise. More than 2,330 Americans were killed, nearly all aircraft on the ground were destroyed and most of the fleet badly damaged. However, three US aircraft carriers were at sea during the attack and survived to form the nucleus of a new fleet. Overall, the attack was only partly successful. It extinguished any remaining desire among Americans to remain neutral, and far from abandoning the Pacific theatre, the USA was determined to exact revenge for Pearl Harbor.

On 8 December 1941 US President Franklin D. Roosevelt called the attack 'a date which will live in infamy'. An hour later the USA formally declared war.

Although troops and sailors from many different countries, especially Australia and New Zealand, fought in the Pacific region, the USA took overall command of the Allied efforts in the South-West Pacific, which became a major theatre of the war following Japan's attack.

Japan's Quest for Empire

December 1941 was a busy month for the Japanese. They continued several offensives: landing in north Malaya, taking Hong Kong, destroying the American air force in the Philippines in another surprise air attack and then landing an invasion force there.

At the south of the Malayan peninsula, British colonial Singapore was supposedly impregnable. The British thought that the jungle protected the city from land attack, so Singapore's massive guns faced out to sea. But its naval powerhouses – a battle cruiser and battleship – were destroyed within one hour of engagement by Japanese bomber planes, and Japanese air attacks caused chaos while their soldiers were hacking their way through the jungle from the north. The Allied troops in Singapore numbered three times that of the Japanese invasion force, but greatly overestimating the Japanese strength (and having underestimated their strategy), British General Percival surrendered in February 1942. It was a humiliation for Britain: the first time that such a huge force had surrendered to such a small one.

The Battle of Midway

Early 1942 saw more Japanese victories. The Philippines, Burma and the Dutch East Indies (Indonesia) – a great prize due to the oil there – all fell. Japan landed elsewhere, including New Guinea and the Solomon Islands to the north of Australia, and the Marshall and Gilbert Islands and Wake Island further north. Japan launched so many bombing raids on northern Australia that women and children were evacuated further south. Then in June, Japan turned its attention to American forces at Midway Island in the middle of the Pacific.

By now Japanese radio communications were being intercepted and American air and naval reinforcements reached Midway in time. The Japanese were repulsed with major losses and from then on Japan didn't win another major battle.

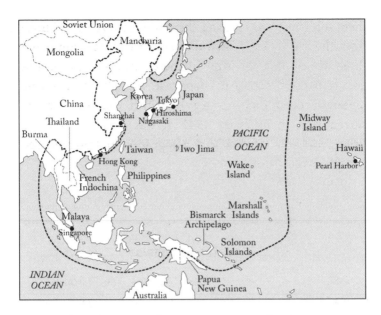

7. The extent of Japanese expansion by 1942.

Quelling the Imperial Dragon

The Allies took the initiative and pressed Japan on several fronts from 1942 onwards. In the South-West Pacific Japan was pushed out of Guadalcanal in the Solomon Islands, and from New Guinea. Allied forces went on to retake the Philippines and, eventually, Okinawa in southern Japan.

In the mid-Pacific a series of amphibious assaults led to what was called 'island-hopping'. Island by island, and often fighting face to face, the Allies gained bases from which to bomb Japan. These forces went on to fight the Battle of Leyte Gulf off the Philippines in October 1944, the largest naval battle in history. The Japanese navy and air force were now powerless to stop the Allies, and in desperation, Japanese suicidal Kamikaze ('divine wind') air attacks were launched. In the meantime, a counter-invasion of Burma led to the liberation of South-East Asia; but still, Japan refused to surrender.

Murder as a Final Solution

Hitler's Nazis had seized power in Germany in 1933 partly by blaming Jews for the country's economic woes (see page 76). His racist philosophy of Aryan superiority claimed that it was Germany's duty to rid the world of 'inferior' races such as the Jews, so from the moment he became Chancellor of the Third Reich in 1933 Hitler enacted anti-Jewish legislation. As fascism took hold, Jewish emigration increased. Among the refugees were Albert Einstein, who left Berlin in 1933, and Sigmund Freud, who abandoned Austria in 1938. Millions more were not so prescient or so lucky.

Jewish businesses and synagogues were attacked on *Kristallnacht* (the 'Night of the Broken Glass') on 9 November 1938. The Nazis began to restrict Jewish emigration, and finally began deporting Jews into ghettos or imprisoning them in concentration camps.

The Nazis' first concentration camp opened in Dachau, Germany, in 1933 to hold political enemies. This category soon extended to include minority groups, particularly Jews but also gypsies and homosexuals. After the war broke out, concentration camps became labour camps, filled with prisoners of war as well as Slavs, Jews and other groups that the Nazis considered to be inferior. Run by the SS, starvation and torture were commonplace in the camps. But there was even worse to come.

In December 1941 the SS opened the first purpose-built death camp, Chelmno in Poland. A month later Nazi leaders met at the Wannsee Conference in Berlin to discuss a 'Final Solution' for what they called the 'Jewish question in Europe'. Their decision was genocide: to establish more extermination camps and annihilate Jews in what became an industrialized process. There were five more death camps, all in Poland, including Auschwitz-Birkenau. Some were so large they had their own train lines. Jewish groups were often told they were being resettled in the east when they were forced onto cattle trucks and taken to a camp, sometimes unloaded directly into the gas chambers. Police officers in occupied countries such as Poland and Vichy France helped round up Jewish people and deport them to camps.

About 6 million Jews were killed (an estimated 78 per cent of Jews in Nazi-occupied Europe) and about 5 million other prisoners died in the death camps during the Holocaust; the worst genocide in history.

Operation Overlord

On 6 June 1944 the first official Allied communication was announced about Operation Overlord: 'Under the command of General Eisenhower, Allied naval forces, supported by strong air forces, began landing Allied armies on the northern coast of France.'

The Allied invasion of Europe had finally begun. Tuesday, 6 June was labelled D-Day, the day when 7,000 boats – the largest armada in history – landed Allied forces on the Normandy beaches and began the liberation of Western Europe. Part of the operation was to convince Germany that the invasion would come further east, at the Pas de Calais. The ruse succeeded, and the German defences were concentrated away from Normandy. Even so, and despite air superiority, the Allies had to struggle against horrific gunfire to establish a beachhead: they suffered about 15,000 casualties at the landing sites.

But within weeks the Allies had broken through the German lines and were driving inland. Paris was liberated on 25 August. As the Soviet Union advanced upon Germany from the east, the Allies passed through Belgium and approached northern Germany. At Arnhem the Allies failed to capture bridges over the Rhine, and in December Hitler launched his last offensive, the Battle of the Bulge, in the Ardennes, where years before he had broken through to France.

The German counter-attack failed, and the Allies advanced into Germany. By April 1944 the Red Army was outside Berlin, and in his bunker Hitler committed suicide on the 30th. Nazi Germany's unconditional surrender followed on 7 May.

Assault of Little Boy and Fat Man

Although there was victory in Europe, Japan stubbornly refused to lose face by admitting defeat. Frustrated, in July 1945 the Allies approved the Potsdam Declaration calling on Japan to surrender or face destruction. Still the Japanese government refused to accept peace. So on 6 August the first atomic bomb, 'Little Boy', was dropped on Hiroshima by an American bomber plane, and three days later a second bomb, 'Fat Man', hit Nagasaki. Thousands of people were killed immediately, and many thousands more died from radiation poisoning. After such a devastating attack, Emperor Hirohito ordered surrender, and finally on 2 September the formal ceremony took place and the war was over.

The atomic bomb, which works by causing a chain reaction within a uranium atom, was based on developments in quantum and nuclear physics that the Nazis had decried as 'degenerate Jewish science'. It was developed in secret by the Manhattan Project in America, and witnessing the test detonation in 1945 Robert Oppenheimer, the scientific head of the project, had quoted from the Hindu scripture the Bhagavad Gita: 'I am become Death, the destroyer of worlds.' The bomb was the biggest project to come out of wartime research but it also showed the way to peaceful uses of nuclear energy. The rockets that would take Apollo II to the moon in 1969 derived directly from the rocket technology that Nazi Germany used to fire V2 bombs during the war.

The Aftermath

When peace was declared Europe was in ruins, with perhaps 6 million displaced persons left homeless in the continent, and millions more refugees in Asia. The destruction of many towns and the new postwar divisions meant that many people would not or could not return to their homes.

Germany and Japan suffered the indignity of occupied zones, the balance of power in the world shifted dramatically from Western Europe to the USA and the USSR (see page 155), new alliances were made and new international groupings were forged. For the first time, war criminals were held to account by the international community.

CHAPTER 5

MID-CENTURY HEYDAY

At the end of the Second World War most of Europe and much of Asia was left economically exhausted. In many countries, industrial bases had been destroyed, and towns and cities needed to be rebuilt. However, US industries had thrived selling military equipment to the Allies, and in 1945 the USA was the world's richest nation, producing 43 per cent of the world's iron ore, 45 per cent of crude steel and 74 per cent of the world's motor vehicles.

Postwar US industrial production began to switch from armaments to consumer goods. It was the beginning of an economic boom that was to affect all except developing countries and last until the mid-1970s.

Europe Rebuilds

As the USSR began to dominate Eastern Europe, the USA launched the Truman Doctrine, a scheme to contain communist power by offering aid – economic, military or political – to any country that the USA feared the Soviets might otherwise influence (see page 156). In 1948 the economic aid became known as the Marshall Plan, named after US Secretary of State George Marshall, through which the USA gave $13 billion to Western European nations to rebuild their economies and engage in free trade. President Truman felt that prosperous nations would be less likely to turn to communism and would help to keep the American economy booming by buying its goods. The USSR prohibited its satellite countries from applying for Marshall aid.

Other institutions aiming to create international financial stability included the Bretton Woods monetary system, set up by the Allied nations in 1944 before the war had ended. Named after the New Hampshire town where the system was forged, it called for member states to fix exchange rates by linking their currencies to the US dollar, which was in turn based on a set amount of gold (the gold standard). The Bretton Woods agreement set up the International Monetary Fund (IMF) to regulate exchange rates and the World Bank to help fund redevelopment. All countries hoped that financial stability with growing worldwide trade would prevent another global war, but the USSR refused to ratify the Bretton Woods agreement, claiming that the USA had too much influence in the IMF and the World Bank and therefore on global finance.

In the 1950s, with the help of the Marshall Plan, rebuilding began to have an effect throughout the nation-members of the North Atlantic Treaty Organization (NATO) and other countries aligned to it (see pages 159–60).

A Shrinking World

While the nineteenth century had been the age of nation-states and empires, a theme of the twentieth century was the formation of international confederations. Some aimed at promoting world peace, others were mutual defence pacts (NATO and the Warsaw Pact) and many were economic trade blocs.

At the end of each of the two traumatic world wars there were attempts at international co-operation: the League of Nations in 1920 and the United Nations (UN) in 1945. The League of Nations was the first international organization specifically aiming to keep world peace, but it proved unable to control the territorial aggression of Germany and the other Axis powers in the 1930s.

In 1946 the League of Nations was dissolved and its assets transferred to a new organization, the United Nations, as agreed by the Allied powers at the Tehran Conference in 1943. The UN came into being in 1945, with fifty-one members including Britain, France, Australia, New Zealand, Canada and the two superpowers, the USSR and the USA. It has had varying degrees of success in its stated purpose 'to maintain international peace and security', but more success in achieving 'international co-operation in solving international problems'.

One of the early acts of the United Nations was to run a conference on trade in 1947 that led to the General Agreement on Tariffs and Trade (GATT). Aiming to regulate and encourage international trade, GATT reduced tariffs and other trade barriers: in 1979 GATT talks between 102 countries resulted in concessions on tariffs worth $190 billion.

GATT was popular because it helped promote growth not only in bigger economies but also in smaller developing economies. In 1995 it evolved into the World Trade Organization, whose purpose remained the promotion of free trade (for more on opening borders for goods see page 207).

Never Had it So Good

Oil prices were low in the 1950s and 1960s enabling all types of industry to flourish. Employment was high; new consumer markets had developed, including markets aimed at children and teenagers (see page 127); and national economies were growing. Although there were slumps, the industrialized nations generally enjoyed financial stability and became wealthier, as did all social classes within those nations. Even Germany and Japan, the countries that were defeated in the war, were part of the boom. It was the golden age of capitalism, sometimes known as the Long Boom. Germans described their economic growth in the 1950s as their 'Economic Miracle', while the boom decades between 1945 and 1975 are known in France as the 'Glorious Thirty'. At the same time, 'Third World' countries – those not aligned to either NATO or its communist opposite, the Warsaw Pact (see page 160) – became poorer.

Technology raced ahead during these years. Industry and agriculture became more efficient through automation and new machines such as combine harvesters, though widespread use of pesticides caused a long-term environmental problem. The 'military economy' based on an arms race and space race caused by the Cold War (see page 155) helped keep the boom going. Although coal was still used in power stations, oil became more and more important to industrialized nations. Alternative sources of energy, including hydraulic, nuclear and gas, were also developing.

In 1957, when the boom was not even at its peak, British Prime Minister Harold Macmillan summed up the new optimism: 'most of our people have never had it so good. Go around the country, go to the industrial towns, go to the farms and you will see a state of prosperity such as we have never had in my lifetime – nor indeed in the history of this country.'

High-rises and Suburbs

Most European countries had seen their housing stock devastated by the Second World War. New homes were needed urgently, and the 'baby boom' (three decades of population growth in the West beginning in the late 1940s) put even more pressure on housing. In 1945 it was estimated that 750,000 new homes were required in England and Wales alone. Some countries responded by building entire new towns, such as Livingston in Scotland and Milton Keynes in England. Most of Europe also built high-rise blocks of flats, often part of new estates on the fringes of towns. Prosperous Americans with their own cars moved by the millions to new suburbs on the periphery of cities: by 1950 more Americans lived in suburbs than in city centres or rural areas.

One solution to the housing crisis was 'prefabs': homes prefabricated in sections that could be assembled quickly and simply on site. Intended to be only a temporary measure, 156,622 prefabs were built in Britain and some are still in use. In 1945 about a quarter of British homes did not have mains electricity, and in 1951 about a third did not have a plumbed-in bath; prefabs, which had not only a bath but an indoor toilet, were a considerable improvement.

After the war the British government continued a policy of clearing slums, the old, overcrowded, unhygienic streets that were deemed unfit for human habitation. By the end of the 1960s about 900,000 slums had been cleared, at least 1.5 million new homes had been built, and 2.5 million people had been rehoused.

The new homes contributed to an enormous increase in individual living standards. Indoor plumbing and electricity became the norm for even poor families, and as the economic boom continued, it also became standard to equip the home with a fridge and a television, and even, eventually, a washing machine.

Busted

A number of factors brought the boom to an end, including the Cold War, which had helped to sustain industry but became increasingly costly to maintain, and oil, which suddenly also became expensive.

In 1971 the US economy was being drained by the Vietnam War (see page 168) and for the first time in five decades was experiencing a balance of trade deficit, when US companies were spending more outside the country than foreign businesses were spending on US goods and services. At the same time, some countries were redeeming their dollars for the fixed rate of gold, devaluing the dollar. President Richard Nixon had to undertake serious measures, and in what is known as the Nixon Shock he withdrew from the Bretton Woods monetary system by breaking the link between the US dollar and gold. It was a politically popular move in America; Nixon's treasury secretary, John Connally, said: 'Foreigners are out to screw us. Our job is to screw them first.' But the collapse of Bretton Woods, replaced by floating exchange rates, led to financial instability: inflation and financial bubbles that offered the hope of growth but then burst.

Oiling the International Wheels

Just as the world was coming to terms with the Nixon Shock, a first oil shock hit the Western world in 1973, when Arab nations placed an oil embargo on the USA and Western Europe for their support of Israel during the Yom Kippur War that year (see page 152), causing oil prices to rise steeply. The oil crisis turned a stock market downturn into a full-scale crash, with the Dow Jones benchmark losing 45 per cent of its value before recovery in December 1974. The knock-on effect was worse in the UK, where the London Stock Exchange went down 73 per cent.

Political and social factors contributed to the downturn. The Watergate scandal (clandestine operations to help re-elect Nixon as US president) was uncovered in June 1972 and culminated in the impeachment of the president for obstruction of justice when he refused to hand over tape recordings made in the White House. In August 1974 Nixon became the only American president to resign.

In the UK, a strike by coal miners in 1973 raised fears of power shortages so the Three-Day Week was introduced by Edward Heath's Conservative government, confining businesses to just three consecutive days of electricity each week and causing blackouts around the country.

The boom was over: unemployment rose, inflation soared and recession hit the West. Meanwhile, oil-producing countries realized that they had enormous power (see page 113).

Tiger Economies Roar

At the end of the Second World War no one thought that Europe would face economic competition from Asia. But Japan was to invade Western households with its cheap electronic consumer goods, ranging from transistor radios to televisions. Japan's electronic miracle, supported by US aid in a programme similar to the postwar Marshall Plan aid (see page 101) the USA offered in Europe, was based on businesses uniting with labour unions to promote full employment. Japan was to become Asia's major economy until Taiwan and Korea evolved into 'tiger economies' in the 1960s. In the 1980s China was to join Asia's growing economic miracle.

Europe Comes Together

At the end of the First World War, the Treaty of Versailles (see page 56) had imposed harsh punitive conditions on Germany, causing economic collapse and resentment that helped fuel the Second World War. In 1945 the victorious Allies were determined to avoid repeating past mistakes. European leaders felt that economic union would help avoid another war: countries that shared joint industries and trading ventures would be unlikely to declare war on each other. Closer links between European countries could also prevent outbreaks of extreme nationalism, such as Nazism; heal the long rift between Germany and France that stretched back to Napoleon's domination of Europe and the Franco-Prussian War; and avoid the economic nationalism of the 1930s when European countries responded to the Great Depression with individual self-interest instead of forging a common response. In defensive terms, Western European nations were now military minnows compared to the giant whales of the USA and the Soviet bloc: they needed to band together.

British politician Winston Churchill said that what was needed was 'a kind of United States of Europe', though he had in mind a customs union and co-operative concept, rather than political union.

Some countries had been planning economic co-operation before the war ended. In 1944 the governments in exile of Belgium, the Netherlands and Luxembourg signed the Benelux Convention to create a future customs union. The 1948 Treaty of Brussels linked Britain and France with the Benelux countries for economic, cultural and military collaboration. Western Europe's military union was funnelled into NATO (see page 159), and in 1948 the Organization for European Economic Co-operation was formed, aiming to make the best possible use of Marshall Plan funds and to encourage trade by reducing restrictions on cross-border trading. It was so successful that in 1961 it expanded by taking in non-European members and became the Organization for Economic Co-operation and Development.

The first tentative steps towards European political integration came in 1948 at the Congress of Europe in The Hague: 750 Western European statesmen attended and called for a European Assembly and a European Court of Human Rights. In May 1949 the Council of Europe was set up, which founded the European Convention for the Protection of Human Rights and the European Court of Human Rights in Strasbourg – not to be confused with the European Court in Luxembourg set up by the European Economic Community (EEC), now the European Union (EU).

An Economic Community Forms

Almost from the end of the Second World War there was tension between France and Germany over control of Germany's steel and coal production. The victorious Allies placed restrictions on Germany's industrial potential but were not prepared to hand over Germany's Ruhr and Rhineland industrial areas to France when the French requested control of the region. As a compromise, federalists proposed that resources should be pooled and administered by common institutions. The resulting European Coal and Steel Community was launched in 1952 with six members: France, West Germany, Italy, Belgium, the Netherlands and Luxembourg. Wider economic co-operation came at the Treaty of Rome in 1957, which set up the European Economic Community in 1958. The EEC offered a common market and no trade restrictions, but went further, proposing to improve living conditions, maintain peace and promote a closer union of European peoples. Within five years the EEC was the world's biggest exporter and purchaser of raw materials, and was second only to the USA as a steel producer. A common agricultural policy was established in 1952.

Britain had refused to join, fearing loss of sovereignty and control. But by 1961 the British economy was stagnating while EEC members' economies were still growing, so Britain applied to join the EEC. In 1963 French President Charles de Gaulle vetoed Britain's application and did so again in 1967. It was only after de Gaulle had resigned that Britain joined the EEC, in 1973.

One of de Gaulle's objections to British entry was that Britain wanted concessions for Commonwealth nations. These concessions were never agreed and gradually Commonwealth countries began to forge close links with their own regional trade communities.

One Currency, One Border

After Western European nations formed the European Economic Community (now absorbed into the European Union), the next stage in integration was the 1992 Maastricht Treaty, which created the European Union. The Maastricht Treaty introduced a single currency (the euro), opened borders within Treaty countries, and moved towards closer immigration and judicial affairs. Two decades later the EU received the Nobel Prize for Peace for its efforts to keep peaceful relations and advance democracy and human rights in Europe.

The EU typified a trend of the twentieth century: away from nationhood and towards large, supranational economic unions. Although there was rivalry and some vicious disputes between countries within the EU, European integration succeeded in its aim of preventing war between member states.

However, since the first moves towards union some people worried about loss of sovereignty, immigration,

8. The European Union in 1999.

the cost and bureaucracy of the European Parliament and other features of political federation. Britain, for example, stayed out of the euro and the open borders Schengen agreement, and in June 2016 Britain's concerns would lead to a referendum on EU membership in which the British people voted to leave the EU.

Culture Clash

As the twentieth century wore on it became clear that oil was no ordinary commodity, but an absolute necessity for industrialized, developed countries. Control of oil was to lead to international conflict and even wars.

It was a British company (Anglo-Iranian Oil) that first found oil in the Middle East (in Iran), and because the region had come under European influence after the First World War it was Western companies that led the search for more oil, developed infrastructure and took the lion's share of the profits. In 1951 Iran became the first Middle Eastern country to become resentful over this arrangement, resulting in nationalization of the Iranian oil industry. Britain led an international boycott and in 1954 Iran reached a compromise, taking a 50 per cent share of the profits from the international oil company.

Other Middle Eastern nations followed suit, demanding a greater share of the profits. Until North Sea oil became available in the 1970s, Europe was dependent upon Middle Eastern oil; previously poor and undeveloped Arab countries became rich on the profits and globally influential.

With raised prices in the 1970s, Middle Eastern oil nations became not just rich but fabulously wealthy.

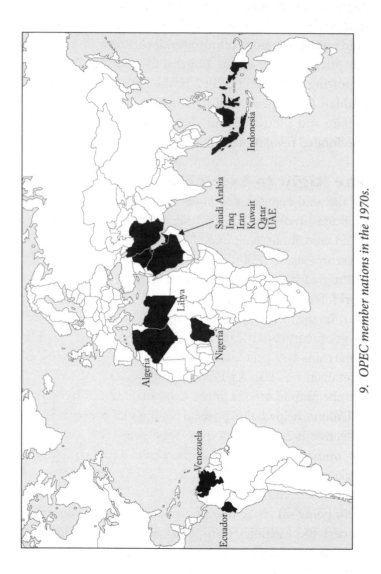

9. OPEC member nations in the 1970s.

Nigeria, which had suppressed the Biafran move to independence from 1967 to 1970 (see page 147) in order to hold on to the region's oil, also saw its fortunes rise through the pricing policy of the Organization of the Petroleum Exporting Countries (OPEC) in the 1970s. Under Colonel Gaddafi, Libya spent some of its oil money on infrastructure, welfare and industrial and agricultural development, but also funded revolutionaries in Africa.

The Right to Assemble

By the mid-century, economies were also being affected by trade unions, which had become so strong that they could contribute to economic crises and help bring down governments.

Progressive ideas of workers' rights had spread as the workforce became better educated after the Second World War. In the USA a GI bill gave war veterans the chance to go to university, an opportunity few working-class Americans had previously enjoyed. So the golden age of capitalism was also a golden age of trade unionism, with membership of unions in the USA peaking in the 1950s.

Unions helped the postwar economic boom through collective bargaining for pay; they supported equal pay for women, opposed racial discrimination and ensured workers' rights such as pensions, redundancy money and employment contracts.

By going on strike unions could affect many aspects of modern life, including transport, rubbish collection, health care, education, the postal service and power supplies. In May 1968 French unions joined student protests against

President Charles de Gaulle's government, paralysing the French economy and forcing de Gaulle to call a snap election. Although de Gaulle was re-elected, May 1968 came to represent the social and cultural revolution that France had witnessed.

Trade unions also had a major impact in Britain in 1978–9 when public sector workers, including ambulance drivers, rubbish collectors and train drivers, went on strike, causing the 'Winter of Discontent'. The resulting social chaos contributed to the defeat in 1979 of the Labour government and an electoral victory for Margaret Thatcher's Conservatives. Britain's first woman prime minister, Thatcher introduced anti-union legislation at a time when British manufacturing industries were in decline, so union action would not have the same power again.

In the 1980s Thatcher's American ally, the Republican US President Ronald Reagan, also weakened unions' powers. Conservative elements in the USA had long feared that unions were a way for communism to enter the country: in 1947 the Taft–Hartley labour management act had barred communists from being union leaders, though this law was later overturned as being unconstitutional.

Democracy for All

While the economic problems of the Great Depression of the 1930s helped fuel fascism (see page 73), the boom years after the Second World War did the opposite, fostering democracy and seeing it spread to much of the world. This political model, which gives every adult a chance to participate in political life by freely electing representatives, came of age in the twentieth century when women gained the vote.

The Suffragette movement for women's votes had started in 1893 when New Zealand became the first country to give women the vote. The impetus towards equal voting rights really began after the First World War (see pages 71–2), when women who had worked in munitions factories, driven ambulances or otherwise helped the war effort could no longer be denied the right to participate in political life. Many countries introduced suffrage for women by the end of the Second World War, though Portugal only ended restrictions on women's voting in 1976, and it was not until 2015 that women in Saudi Arabia were allowed to vote.

In decolonized Africa most newly independent countries adopted the democratic model of their former European colonizers. Japan was influenced to do so by the Allied occupation after the Second World War. Elsewhere in Asia, in 1932 a bloodless coup in Siam (renamed Thailand in 1939) ended the absolute monarchy, forcing the king to allow the first constitution, if not full democracy.

In the 1960s and early 1970s democracy was failing in some parts of the world. Single-party communist states offered only a sham pretence at free elections, electoral corruption was widespread in some regions, and in several former European colonies the democratic system simply overlaid internal divisions, so that presidents who were supported by ethnic, religious or cultural majorities became rulers for life. Military coups resulted in juntas in countries as varied as Burma (by military commander Ne Win in 1962), Greece (the Colonels, 1967), Uganda (1971, by Idi

Amin), Chile (overthrowing Salvador Allende in 1973) and Argentina (overthrowing Isabel Perón in 1976). Later, in 1992, democracy also failed in Algeria when the army deposed the elected Islamic FIS party, fearing that it was too fundamentalist.

Many of these coups or dictatorships were funded by Cold War rivals (see page 156), so as Cold War tensions eased from the late 1970s there were fewer attempted coups or revolutions in Africa and Latin America. Civilian rule was restored in many countries, sometimes as a result of massive demonstrations, as in the Philippines in 1986. With the collapse of communism in Eastern Europe, new nations that had previously formed part of the communist USSR attempted to embrace democracy, with varying degrees of success.

Apartheid Falls in South Africa

In 1948 a member of the South African parliament would have proudly said that the country was a democracy, but this was true only for white citizens. It was the year that the minority white government adopted the policy of racial apartheid: 'separation'. Intended to keep white and black people apart, it meant that black Africans were forced to live in squalid townships outside cities, had few educational opportunities and could not vote.

Popular protests against this discrimination were harshly crushed. In 1960 police fired on demonstrators in Sharpeville, killing sixty-nine, and in 1976 high-school students in Soweto protesting the imposition of the Afrikaans language in schools were also shot at by police. At least 176 people were killed, and in 1977 anti-apartheid leader Steve Biko died in police custody. International protests isolated the country, and Nelson Mandela, the imprisoned leader of the anti-apartheid opposition, the African National Congress, become a focus of global support for the black majority.

Mandela Freed

True democracy arrived in South Africa in a surprise move by President F. W. de Klerk in 1990, when he released Nelson Mandela and helped dismantle apartheid. Mandela and several others had been convicted of crimes against the government in 1964 and sentenced to life imprisonment. During the trial, facing the possibility of a death sentence, Mandela had said: 'During my lifetime I have dedicated myself to this struggle of the African people. I have fought against White domination, and I have fought against Black domination. I have cherished the ideal of a democratic and free society in which all persons will live together in harmony and with equal opportunities. It is an ideal which I hope to live for and to achieve. But if needs be, it is an ideal for which I am prepared to die.'

Dignified and graceful despite twenty-six years of captivity, Mandela presided over a peaceful transition to majority rule and, with black South Africans voting for the first time, was elected the first South African president of the new era in 1994.

Civil Rights in Southern States

While the USA was fighting the Cold War against communism in the 1950s and 1960s to defend its way of life and 'freedom' (see page 155), some US Southern states still denied equality to African-Americans.

Slavery was not banned in the Southern USA until 1863, so some campaigners who worked for African-American civil rights in the post-Second World War era were the grandchildren of slaves. In the 1950s white supremacists of the Ku Klux Klan ran a campaign of terror, including lynchings, to maintain segregation, a policy of keeping white and black people apart. As in South African apartheid, this meant that black Americans had second-rate schools, health care and opportunities.

There were many milestones in the African-American Civil Rights Movement. The Montgomery Bus Boycott began in 1955 when seamstress Rosa Parks was arrested for refusing to give up her bus seat to a white man, so African-Americans boycotted the bus service. Despite a Supreme Court ruling that schools and universities should be integrated, there were violent protests when black students tried to enrol. In 1963 the Baptist minister Martin Luther King, who espoused non-violent civil disobedience to achieve civil rights goals, made his inspirational 'I have a dream' speech. Malcolm X, another important civil rights leader, was assassinated by rivals in 1965.

Full democracy finally arrived in the USA in 1965 with the Voting Rights Act, which meant that African-Americans in the South could vote without fear of intimidation.

Aboriginal Rights in Australia

The 1960s also saw democracy extend to all citizens of Australia. Until 1962 Aboriginal people in several parts of the country could not vote in federal elections unless they were ex-servicemen, but a new law that year extended the vote to all indigenous people, though it took three more years before they were given the vote in Queensland's state elections.

Before the decade was out Australia also dismantled the 'White Australia Policy', which effectively barred immigration from anywhere other than Western Europe and was aimed particularly at restricting immigration from Asia. A 'points' system for would-be migrants was introduced instead, reflecting skills and economic background.

Like some other countries, in the 1960s the Australian government was still taking indigenous children from their homes and putting them in state boarding schools, a policy that only ended in the 1970s but which later drew a formal apology from the state.

Rights and Freedoms

In Victorian Britain children had worked up to eighteen hours a day in dangerous conditions in mines and factories or cleaning chimneys. Children had no right to social or special protection.

The groundbreaking United Nations Universal Declaration of Human Rights in 1948 granted these rights to children, along with all other sectors of society. The declaration accepted that humans have some inalienable rights: to safety, food and shelter; protection;

equal treatment; and, in the case of adults, the right to a democratic vote. In 1949 the Geneva Convention added that prisoners of war should be treated humanely.

During the latter part of the twentieth century the rights movement expanded to condemn the abuse of children by religious institutions, to explore animal rights, to encompass prisoners and to promote ethical consumerism.

Protective Arm of the State

The twentieth century witnessed a social revolution as some nations created mechanisms to provide help for all from the cradle to the grave. Unlike previous charitable institutions that might have offered help only within a certain geographical area or to certain types of people, these new welfare systems became available equally to everyone.

Perhaps the basis of the modern European welfare state was German Chancellor Otto von Bismarck's ideas for social reforms from as early as the 1840s, including old-age pensions, accident insurance and medical care. Bismarck had hoped to pre-empt social unrest and reduce emigration from the German Empire to the USA. His ideas influenced many European nations to begin some form of social insurance for workers during the early part of the twentieth century.

In the USA, the hotbed of capitalism, wages were relatively high but there was no state support for individuals. US businesses and conservatives were opposed to state involvement. When the Great Depression struck in the 1930s (see page 70), the USA was the only industrialized nation not to have an insurance scheme for its workers, which meant that families made destitute by the lack of work had to rely upon limited charitable resources to survive. President Herbert Hoover felt that the state had no part to play in social relief, but his successor in 1933, Franklin D. Roosevelt, initiated the New Deal, a series of programmes to provide jobs and give workers some rights. In 1935 he introduced the Social Security Act, which set up unemployment insurance, agricultural subsidies, state care for the disabled and for some children, and offered pensions to some workers. But the USA did not have a health-care programme: by the early twenty-first century its infant mortality rate of 5 per cent was higher than most European nations, and also higher than in Cuba, its ideological enemy for much of the twentieth century.

In France, modern social services began with the Matignon Accords of 1936 when a union strike forced the government and employers to guarantee workers' rights such as holidays and a forty-hour working week.

In Britain, the Beveridge Report by economist William Beveridge proposed ways to counter five 'Giant Evils' in society: squalor, ignorance, want, idleness and disease. As a result, from 1944 to 1948 Britain created the 'Welfare State', introducing National Insurance, whereby workers paid in to a system that gave them sickness and unemployment benefits, and the National Health Service (NHS), giving free health services to all, regardless of means.

A Quiet Revolution

The postwar economic prosperity and feelings of social optimism spurred many countries into moving social services away from private, often religious, charities into state control. Canada's Quiet Revolution took place in the province of Quebec in the 1960s, when the government took control of health care and education, previously run by the Roman Catholic Church, and began a universal pension plan creating a welfare state.

Several systems of social assistance developed around the world. In Denmark, Norway, Sweden, Iceland and Finland the so-called Nordic model created a comprehensive socialist welfare state along with free-market capitalism. Middle Eastern oil-producing countries kept their wealth within the country by giving benefits only to their own citizens and denying citizenship to foreign workers. China went its own way and shocked the world in 1978 by introducing a one-child policy to try to curb population growth and relieve pressure on government resources. It succeeded in this aim, but caused a skewed population, as millions of baby girls were abandoned (or even killed) so that families could have a son. It is estimated that men outnumber women by about 33 million in China today.

Medical Milestones

With the introduction of state-supported services such as Britain's National Health Service, medicine entered the political realm, and began to be incorporated into capitalist systems with the growth of health insurance, influential pharmaceutical companies and even the test-tube baby industry.

Technology became an important feature of medicine in the latter half of the twentieth century, building on earlier developments such as kidney dialysis machines, invented in 1943, and EEGs (electroencephalograms) measuring electrical activity in the brain, which were first carried out on humans in 1929. The first internal artificial pacemaker was implanted in 1958, and the late 1950s saw the introduction of life-support machines such as modern ventilators, replacing the huge iron-lung machines of the 1930s. The first heart transplant was carried out in 1967, after which organ transplants became routine operations.

Although medical technology was partly responsible for people (in the Western world at least) living longer and healthier lives, simple improvements in hygiene had a major effect, as did advances in disease prevention, such as the polio vaccine introduced in 1955. And after decades of effort, smallpox – which killed between 300 million and 500 million people in the twentieth century – was declared eradicated in 1980.

Despite all the advances, drugs such as thalidomide, marketed in the 1950s as a sedative safe for pregnant women and causing thousands of babies worldwide to be born with malformed limbs, were a reminder that research can go wrong, providing an incentive for rigorous testing of new drugs.

Care in the Community

At the beginning of the century anyone suffering from mental health issues was considered to be sick, and very likely would be locked up in an asylum where outdated treatments such as lobotomies were practised. A major change took place from the 1950s onwards as psychiatric hospitals were merged with general hospitals: instead of incarceration, patients were given care in the community. The new approach to patients tried to remove the stigma attached to mental illness. By the 1960s a range of better psychotropic drugs became available, and older, potentially dangerous treatments such as electroconvulsive shock therapy were considered to be unhelpful, if not barbaric. The trend in the latter part of the century towards better treatment of the mentally ill was part of the overall improvement in medical care, and also part of the movement towards civil rights in every aspect of life, in this case patients' rights.

The March to Miniaturization

In 1946 the first electronic computer weighed 30 tons, filled a room and was powered by thousands of vacuum tubes. A few decades later it would be unusual for an individual not to have a personal computer (PC) and mobile phone.

The invention of the microchip or integrated circuit in the 1950s made computers smaller and more powerful. In 1981 US company IBM launched the first PC, with Apple introducing the Macintosh in 1984. Computers started to transform much of life, from work to shopping and socializing.

Microchips grew out of the groundbreaking invention of transistors in 1947, where a low electric current is applied to a small chip of silicon. First used in telecommunications, individual transistors in the late 1950s were integrated onto a single piece of silicon to form a full circuit (microchip, or chip). As the chips became more powerful and their programming more sophisticated, they would be used in everything from credit cards to ID chips implanted in pets.

Let's Twist: Media and Pop Culture

As the twentieth century began, France was the cultural centre of the Western world. Spanish artist Pablo Picasso, American dancer Josephine Baker and many others gravitated there to make their names. But by the 'Long Boom' (see page 104), the period of economic growth following the Second World War, it was American culture that influenced the world, not least through the new visual media of films and television.

Cinema from the 1910s had become the first form of industrialized mass entertainment and most people in Western countries regularly visited the cinema. From 1912 Hollywood in Los Angeles became the centre for American film studios. During the First World War the studios worked with the US government on war propaganda, then in the 1920s clever marketing and their financial power helped them dominate the international film industry, bringing American ideas of society and politics into every country.

Just as celebrity culture grew, the profits from film-making rose. A silent movie of the 1920s might have made about $10 million at the box office. But in 1960 Alfred Hitchcock's film *Psycho* earned more than $40 million, while the top-earning film of the 1970s (1977's *Star Wars*) earned $147 million. The billion-dollar barrier would be broken in 1997 by *Titanic*. By then, videos, DVDs and video games were also generating profits of millions, if not billions, of dollars.

One of the most dramatic social changes of the twentieth century was the development of mass media that reached into homes. First radio and then television made news, ideas and culture instantly accessible, and all forms of media became more sophisticated and manipulative. Disasters always make great headlines, and eyewitness reporting of the *Hindenburg* Disaster in 1937, when the airship caught fire, showed the news industry that it had enormous power to influence the public.

In 1954 the small, portable transistor radio was introduced along with vinyl records. Youth culture exploded. Fashion, music and dance styles aimed specifically at young people spread around the world, with the young adopting slang expressions that were meant to exclude the older generation.

One trend of twentieth-century music was the growing influence of African-American styles. From the ragtime of the early century through the blues of poor, rural Southern black people and the jazz of urban African-Americans, the styles were picked up by white performers. In the 1950s black and white music continued to come together in rock and roll, when Elvis Presley destroyed the idea that singers should just stand still and croon, and Little Richard played to desegregated audiences.

In Britain, teen culture became more influential in the 'Swinging Sixties' as bands such as The Beatles, The Rolling Stones and The Who broke into the American market and became famous around the world. Pop music began to develop into a host of genres, including punk rock and hip-hop.

In addition to the growth in youth culture, the 1960s was a period of rapid social change. A new wave of feminism was coupled with the introduction of the contraceptive pill, giving women more freedom than ever before. At the same time, young people in the Western world explored alternative lifestyles in the 'counterculture'. Hippies embraced psychoactive drugs and 'ethnic' arts, particularly jewellery and clothing, from African and Asian countries, and for the first time atheism and secularism became commonplace in the West. Despite the trend towards secularism and realism, the literary bestsellers of the twentieth century were fantasies: J. R. R. Tolkien's *The Lord of the Rings* (published in 1954 and selling over 150 million copies) and J. K. Rowling's *Harry Potter and the Philosopher's Stone* (published in 1997, selling over 120 million copies).

CHAPTER 6

END OF COLONIALISM

After the Second World War, the European colonial expansion that had peaked in the 'Scramble for Africa' (see page 13) was reversed. Decolonization began with India, the jewel in the British Empire's crown, and spread to Africa.

African anti-colonial movements were formed by indigenous peoples angry about settlers exploiting their land and eroding their culture. The Maji Maji uprising in the colony of German East Africa, from 1905 to 1907, was a tragic example of the imbalance of power. When the indigenous Africans rebelled against the German colonials they believed they would be protected by a 'war medicine' that turned bullets into water (*maji* in Kiswahili), and many thousands died as a consequence. This colony, like others belonging to powers defeated in the First World War, would become a mandate administered by the Allies. It achieved independence in the 1960s as Burundi, Rwanda and Tanzania.

Anti-colonialist movements in other colonies gained momentum after the Second World War, triggering the break-up of the Japanese, Italian, British, French,

Dutch, Portuguese and Belgian empires. The transition to independence for some colonies, such as British Malaya in South-East Asia, was relatively peaceful. In others, for example those with many settlers owning large, prosperous tracts of land such as British Kenya, Portuguese Angola and British Southern Rhodesia (now Zimbabwe) in Africa, it took an armed uprising to persuade colonial powers to withdraw. Dismantling the colonial empires caused mass movements of people and left a legacy of political, social and economic instability.

Steps towards Decolonization

After the First World War US President Woodrow Wilson urged democratic nations to stop territorial expansion into other countries, believing that people should enjoy the right to self-determination and to govern themselves. Colonies of the war's losing empires were distributed among victorious nations as mandates, the governing of which was to be supervised by the League of Nations, a forerunner of the United Nations (see page 103), until the mandate populations were ready 'to stand by themselves under the strenuous conditions of the modern world'. Although the mandates were not equal to independence, the political agenda leading to self-government in these countries had been set.

Britain and France received mandates in the Middle East from the Ottoman Empire (see page 58) together with parts of the Cameroons and Togoland in West Africa. Belgium administered a mandated part of German East Africa. German islands in the North and South Pacific Oceans were divided between Japan, Australia and New Zealand. The Union of South Africa (a British dominion, which became the Republic of South Africa in 1961) received German South-West Africa (now Namibia).

By 1947 the mandate system had ended and Iraq, Syria, Lebanon and Jordan had become independent countries. The remaining mandates continued to be administered by the countries to which they had been allocated but the United Nations took over the supervisory role until these territories were ready for independence.

For other colonies, the turning point for independence movements came at the end of the Second World War. By this time, traditionally agricultural colonies that had diversified into industry, including India and parts of West Africa, had a new, educated middle class who organized national liberation movements.

British Raj in Crisis

The British Empire, comprising dominions, colonies, protectorates and mandates around the globe and holding sway over one-fifth of the world's population at its height, had become a potential economic burden following the Second World War. Though on the winning side, Britain was bankrupt, kept afloat by loans from the USA. Money spent on fighting independence movements was a luxury the British could no longer afford. This led Britain to pursue a policy of disengagement from its colonies under Clement Attlee's new Labour government of 1945.

Opposition to British rule in India up to 1900 had been limited. India had supplied Britain with raw materials, a market for British manufactured goods (one-fifth of all British exports went to India), and huge numbers of soldiers in two world wars. Many Indians hoped their loyal service would lead to home rule and felt let down when their national government remained firmly in the hands of the British Raj (British Crown rule in India).

Hampering independence was tension between Indian Hindus and Muslims, aggravated by the 1905 separation of Bengal province into Hindu and Muslim areas by Viceroy Curzon, the British governor in India. The Hindu minority in Muslim East Bengal complained of intimidation by Muslims, but Britain refused to reverse the partition, leading to a boycott of British goods and rioting. By 1909 the British had introduced reforms including local 'legislatures' elected by Indian people, but with only 2 per cent of Indians allowed to vote (the most wealthy and best educated) the reforms were not enough. A massacre of Indians by British soldiers at a demonstration in the holy city of Amritsar in 1919 galvanized Indian opponents to British rule into action.

At the same time, liberal democratic ideas spreading among Hindus, who called for more rights and better living standards, were causing unease among wealthier Muslims. Indian Hindu nationalist leader and champion of the poor Mahatma Gandhi led non-violent campaigns supporting Indian independence and the lowest caste of Indian society, the 'untouchables'. Gandhi envisioned India as a democratic republic in which all Indians, regardless of class or religion, would live in harmony.

Salt Shakes the Empire

In 1930 Gandhi led a non-violent twenty-four day 'Salt March' from Sabermati (near Ahmadabad) to the Arabian Sea, a journey of 388 kilometres (240 miles) to protest against repressive British salt taxes in India. With thousands of his followers, Gandhi arrived on the coast where he collected a lump of sea salt from the beach, thereby violating the salt laws, and declared: 'With this, I am shaking the foundations of the British Empire.' Gandhi was arrested but released after his imprisonment sparked protests. Following Gandhi's example, Indians began producing their own salt; 100,000 were arrested by the end of the year and industries were paralysed by strike action.

Gandhi's civil disobedience using non-violent methods was a turning point in India's fight for independence. In 1931 he was invited to talks in London to discuss Indian self-rule. Although no settlement was found at this meeting that would satisfy the Hindus, Muslims and British, Gandhi had attracted worldwide media attention to India's plight and loosened Britain's control over India.

Quit India

In 1942 Gandhi and Indian National Congress leader Jawaharlal Nehru launched a 'Quit India' movement timed to upset the British war effort. Indians united behind the movement until 1947, when the National Congress refused a proposal by India's Muslim League to create a separate Islamic state of Pakistan (meaning 'Land of the Pure') in the event of India's independence. The disagreement caused riots between Hindus and Muslims. Gandhi tried to stop the fighting but 4,000 people were killed.

Less than a month later, the new Viceroy of India, Lord Louis Mountbatten, announced plans to partition British India into two new sovereign dominions of India and Pakistan, separating Hindus from Muslims, plans that were realized in August 1947. Predominantly Hindu West Bengal became part of India and predominantly Muslim East Bengal became a province of Pakistan, known as East Pakistan, and gained independence as Bangladesh in 1971 following a nationalist war of liberation.

The 1947 Partition of India generated chaos as millions of displaced Muslims and Hindus tried to reach the new borders. Hundreds of thousands died and Gandhi was killed in the violence, shot by a Hindu extremist opposed to Gandhi's mission to bring harmony between Hindus and Muslims. Three years later, in 1950, the dominion of India gained full independence from Britain, adopting its own constitution. Pakistan adopted its own constitution in 1956.

The British left India a divided nation. The leader of the Muslim League, Muhammad Jinnah, described the birth of Pakistan and India as being 'drowned in blood'. Following independence, conflict between the two republics continued with wars and skirmishes. Today, the Republic of India, despite great poverty, is the world's largest democracy with significant civil liberties and a free press. Pakistan, a parliamentary republic, has less poverty but has suffered political instability and terrorism (see page 194).

From Empire to Commonwealth

Six months after the partition of India, the island colony of British Ceylon (now Sri Lanka), famed for its tea, gained independence from Britain in 1948, having drawn inspiration from the Quit India campaign. British Malaya, rich in rubber and tin, and occupied by the Japanese during the war, became a British protectorate in 1948. It gained independence in 1957 and was renamed Malaysia in 1963.

Ceylon, India, Pakistan and Malaya became members of the Commonwealth, set up in 1949 with the British monarch at its head as a free association of independent states, mostly former territories of the British Empire, all committed to equality, democracy, world peace and free trade. By the 1950s British trade with Commonwealth nations was four times higher than British trade with Europe, though the balance was to shift when Britain joined the European bloc in 1973. Currently, the Commonwealth comprises fifty-three countries; the four largest economies, the United Kingdom, India, Canada and Australia, make up nearly a third of the world's population.

Green Line Divides Cyprus

The British colony of Cyprus (formerly part of the Ottoman Empire and controlled by Britain from 1878 after the Russo-Turkish War) also joined the Commonwealth after gaining independence from the British Empire in

1960. Tensions between the island's Greek Cypriot majority and the Turkish Cypriot minority led to segregation of the two communities and violence when Greek Cypriots campaigned to unify with mainland Greece. British and United Nations forces were drawn in to monitor the situation. In 1974 the Cypriot government was toppled in a military coup and the president replaced by an activist for Greek union, prompting Turkey to occupy northern Cyprus.

A peace deal in 1974 partitioned Cyprus into a northern third (the Turkish Republic of Northern Cyprus) and a southern two-thirds (the Republic of Cyprus, inhabited by Greek Cypriots), divided by a 'Green Line', a United Nations buffer zone. To this day the Turkish Republic of Northern Cyprus is recognized only by Turkey as an independent country.

Suez Debacle

Egypt, part of the Ottoman Empire until 1914 when it became a British protectorate, gained independence in 1922 following a revolution. Britain maintained an army presence to control the Suez Canal, which was still owned by an Anglo-French company. The waterway through Egypt was vital for bringing Gulf oil to Europe.

In 1952 a revolution led by Egyptian nationalist army officers deposed the pro-British Egyptian King Farouk and declared Egypt a republic in 1953. Gamal Abdel Nasser, president from 1956, shocked the world by nationalizing the Suez Canal to raise funds for a dam project. Crisis talks in London attended by twenty-two nations found no diplomatic solution, so Britain, France and Israel agreed a secret plan to invade Egypt. The invasion in October 1956, led by Israeli forces, was backed by British and French air strikes. Nasser retaliated by blocking the Suez Canal and sinking forty-seven ships there, leading to petrol rationing in Europe. After a week's fighting, the USA, the USSR and the UN forced the invaders to withdraw.

The Suez Crisis caused the resignation of British Prime Minister Anthony Eden, marked the end of Britain's role as a major world power and contributed in 1960 to a UN resolution calling on countries to give up their remaining colonies.

Setting the Stage for Vietnam

France had ruled territory between India and China, known as French Indochina, since France's 1887 victory in the Sino-French War (1884–5). Southern Vietnam (then called Cochinchine) became a French colony while Cambodia (Cambodge), Laos and central and northern Vietnam (Tonkin and Annam) were French protectorates (protected from military invasion). The French exploited the area for rubber, tea, coffee, rice and pepper crops, and were generally resented by the local population.

After the fall of France during the Second World War, the Vichy French government (a puppet state of Nazi Germany – see page 83) handed control of Vietnamese cities Hanoi and Saigon to Japan, Nazi Germany's wartime ally. Imperial Japan had ambitions to take control of Asia and was in the throes of a full-scale war against China (1937–45) (see page 91): soon Japan had occupied all of French Indochina, replacing French officials with Japanese.

At the close of the Second World War in 1945, defeated Japan withdrew from Vietnam, leaving the Viet Minh (League for the Liberation of Vietnam), who had fought Japanese occupation, to seize Hanoi and proclaim a Democratic Republic of Vietnam. The republic was short-lived as French forces returned to re-establish control, retaking Hanoi and forcing the Viet Minh, led by nationalist/communist Ho Chi Minh, to retreat to the mountains. The Viet Minh fought a guerrilla war against France from 1946.

In 1949 the French installed a puppet Vietnamese king, Bao Dai, to undermine Ho Chi Minh, but the communist-led Viet Minh was about to get stronger. China, now the communist People's Republic of China (see page 175), sent military support to the guerrilla fighters, who used bicycles to carry artillery gun pieces into the hills for a surprise attack on the French-held garrison Dien Bien Phu in 1954. Defeated and humiliated, the French withdrew from Indochina.

The USA, where President Harry Truman's 'Containment' policy aimed to stop the spread of communism, had supported France's struggle. Dwight Eisenhower, president from 1953, described the threat as a domino effect whereby if one country fell to communism, the rest of South-East Asia would follow.

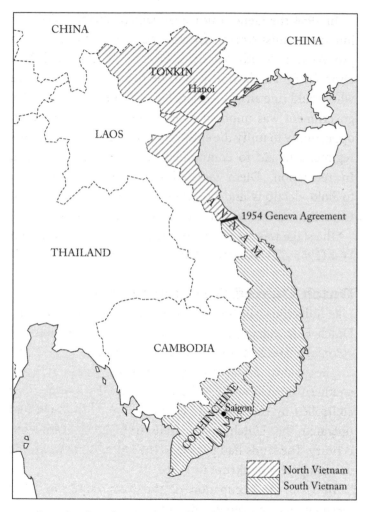

10. *French colonial territories in South-East Asia (Indochina) and the setting for the Vietnam War.*

In 1954 the Geneva peace agreement divided Vietnam into communist North Vietnam, led by Ho Chi Minh, and pro-Western South Vietnam led by US-appointed Ngo Dinh Diem; an election was to be held in 1956 to decide who would rule all of Vietnam. Ngo Dinh Diem's repressive government was unpopular and Ho Chi Minh, seeing an opportunity to unify the entire country under a communist regime, sent aid to communist supporters in the south. In retaliation, Diem violated the Geneva requirement to hold elections and the USA, concerned to show that Containment was working, upheld Diem's decision.

The stage was set for the protracted and costly Vietnam War (1955–75) (see page 168).

Dutch Ousted from East Indies

Like Indochina, the South-East Asian colony known as the Dutch East Indies (now Indonesia) resisted the return of colonial power after the Second World War.

The colony, an archipelago including Sumatra, Java, southern Borneo and Celebes, was formed from territory controlled by the Dutch East India Company, which had operated the Dutch spice trade from the seventeenth century. The lands had passed to the Dutch state when the company went bankrupt in 1796.

In 1940 the occupation of the Netherlands by Nazi Germany had prevented the Dutch army from defending its colony, which was invaded by Japan. The Japanese armed and trained the Indonesians to fight in the war effort against Western Allied forces and encouraged the growth of nationalist movements. The nationalist leaders then claimed Indonesian independence on Japan's surrender at the end of the war.

During five chaotic years from 1945 the Dutch tried to reimpose their rule. Republicans, communists and rural revolutionaries struggled with each other and against the Europeans. Finally, pressure from the United Nations and the USA persuaded the Netherlands to grant independence to Indonesia in 1949.

Heart of Darkness

After the Second World War only three African countries were independent: Liberia, Egypt and Ethiopia. While many Africans had fought for European armies, most were excluded from governing their own countries. Relations between colonists and Africans were generally poor, with atrocities committed most infamously by Belgian King Leopold II (reigned 1865–1909), whose murderous regime governing the rubber-rich, rainforested Congo was the basis for Joseph Conrad's 1899 novel *Heart of Darkness*. Drawing strength from India's new-found freedom, a great wave of independence was to sweep across the African continent during the 1960s.

Ghana in the British Gold Coast was the first African colony to win independence in this period. Gold Coast soldiers who had fought alongside the British in the Second World War returned home to find unemployment and poverty. Tensions escalated when several were shot dead by British colonial officers during a riot, leading Britain to make plans to exit the colony. With British support, Kwame Nkrumah won the country's first election in 1951 and became prime minister in 1957 when Ghana gained independence. Nkrumah began with high hopes of developing an industrialized socialist state with educational opportunities for all, but Ghana suffered economic crisis and under Nkrumah became a one-party state. Nkrumah was ousted in a military coup in 1966.

Ghana's independence inspired other African nations to take control, including Kenya, where attacks by a militant nationalist group, the Mau Mau, on British settler farmers led first to a British backlash including repressive policies, then rebellion and finally to Kenyan independence in 1963.

Prime Minister Harold Macmillan admitted in 1960: 'The wind of change is blowing through the continent . . . the growth of national consciousness is a political fact and we must take account of it.'

Cold Wind Blows in Africa

Decolonization of Africa was complicated by the Cold War struggle between the USA and the USSR (see page 155). The Soviet Union supplied arms and money to nationalist movements driven by communist ideals while the USA, committed to stopping the spread of communism, promoted nationalist groups and leaders who supported the capitalist West.

The rivalry was exemplified by the transfer of independence to the troubled Belgian Congo. Faced with a strengthening pro-independence movement, King Baudouin of Belgium handed over power in 1960 to a newly elected prime minister, the Congolese revolutionary leader Patrice Lumumba. Within two weeks the army had mutinied against the remaining Belgian officers, and the province of Katanga had declared independence from Congo under pro-Western leader Moise Tshombe, who called the Belgians back for military support. Lumumba reacted by requesting the expulsion of Belgian troops by the United Nations, which deployed a force to keep the peace. Lumumba then took military aid from the Soviet Union, which was readily supplied in a communist bid for the Congo, but by September 1960 Lumumba had been driven out and executed by pro-Western Joseph Mobutu (Mobutu Sese Seko). Supported by America, Mobutu became leader in 1965, renaming the country Zaire. He was eventually ousted in 1996 by which time the state had become corrupt and virtually bankrupt.

Angola, struggling for independence from Portugal (1961–75), similarly received Soviet military support (see page 148), and so did the newly independent government of Mozambique and the African National Congress in South Africa. In retaliation, the USA provided weapons and money to African nationalists and governments prepared to oppose communism.

The Soviets did not achieve the results in Africa they had hoped for. Weak economies and violent rivalries created political instability that prevented socialism from taking hold in Africa, and unlike in socialist countries, class struggle was not a primary concern in African societies. Post-independence, most African countries eventually sided with the capitalist West.

Savagery on All Sides

Shamed by the 1954 defeat in French Indochina (see page 139), the socialist French government made a futile bid to hold on to its French Algerian colony of 130 years. France's war there against Arab nationalist guerrilla group Front de Libération Nationale (FLN), between 1954 and 1962, was to come to another humiliating end, the repercussions of which still echo in France today.

The relatively affluent European settlers in Algeria (about 10 per cent of the population) were nicknamed 'Pieds-Noirs' ('black-foots') by native Algerians, who were increasingly discontented and wanted the same rights as the Pieds-Noirs. The French government complied with only limited reforms, fuelling the establishment of reactionary groups like the FLN.

War erupted and lasted eight savage years: the FLN committed massacres, murder, mutilation and torture; the French responded with vicious treatment of nationalist agitators. The conflict brought down France's weak Fourth Republic, replacing it with the Fifth Republic headed up by Charles de Gaulle, who had led Free France during the Second World War. De Gaulle found no alternative but to hand over power to the FLN and grant Algeria independence. The decision led to terrorist acts by French Algerians opposed to independence and within a year 1.4 million refugees, including Europeans and Jews who had resided in Algeria for generations, fled to France where many felt alienated, a problem felt to this day.

Winds of Change

Following independence many of Africa's new nation-states plunged into political and economic chaos. African economies based on subsistence agriculture with few modern industries floundered after the sudden loss of Western support. Countries with valuable raw materials, for example Nigeria's oil reserves, experienced rapid economic growth, creating a gap between rich and poor. Governments faced with multiple problems, from war and ethnic division to famine and drought, tended towards autocracy and corruption for survival.

Infighting in Algeria following the exit of the French resulted in a military dictatorship. The country descended into civil war in the 1990s, when the government cancelled elections fearing an Islamist government would win. However, in recent years Algeria has maintained stability, and become a significant exporter of natural gas.

After gaining independence from France, which had ruled in the region from the nineteenth century until 1960, the Central African Republic suffered autocratic leaders, including the reign of terror by dictator Jean-Bédel Bokassa from 1966 until he was overthrown in a coup supported by France in 1979. The country remains one of the poorest in the world.

In 1971 Idi Amin, an ex-officer of the British colonial army, seized power in the former British protectorate of Uganda, which had already experienced years of corrupt government. Amin brought his own brutal brand of oppressive and cruel government that lasted until 1979, known for executions of political dissenters, gross human rights abuses and ethnic violence. Today the country has attained relative stability and prosperity, though it still suffers from poverty in the north where there is a legacy of unrest and violence caused by the rebel group, the Lord's Resistance Army.

Nigeria, decolonized by the British in 1960, plunged into civil war when Biafra in the south, inhabited by mainly Christian Igbo people, split off from the northern Muslim-dominated federation, creating the Republic of Biafra in 1967, which lasted until 1970. The Biafrans' republic failed after a military blockade by the federal government caused famine and the death of millions of starving Biafrans. International interest and military support on both sides was considerable due to the high-quality oil fields in this region. Images of desperate Biafrans posted around the world drew a flood of humanitarian aid from 1968, particularly from Christian organizations.

Oil also changed the fortunes of former Italian colony Libya. Granted independence in 1951 following Allied occupation, the oil reserves discovered in 1959 were an incentive for the military coup by Colonel Muammar Gaddafi in 1969. However, while Libya's income from oil soared in the 1970s, much of it was spent on sponsoring terrorism around the world (see page 195).

Revolution of Carnations

The Portuguese colony of Angola in southern Africa was known for slave-trading until 1836. The colony had become increasingly Westernized during the twentieth century, but Portugal from 1910 had grown volatile after its failed constitutional monarchy was replaced by an unstable republic, which in turn was superseded in 1933 by a repressive, fascist dictatorship, the Estado Novo ('new state'), fiercely opposed to communism, socialism, liberalism and anti-colonialism. The Estado Novo wanted to make Portugal's colonial possessions part of Portugal itself and ignored all demands for independence from its overseas territories.

Estado Novo policies in Angola, including forced labour and involuntary relocations during the 1950s, sparked a War of Liberation involving several nationalist guerrilla movements and terrible massacres over thirteen years. The Portuguese, struggling to contain the conflict, attracted criticism from the United Nations, arms embargoes and other sanctions imposed by the inter-national community.

Escalating dissent and the rise of Soviet influence among the Portuguese working class led to Portugal's Carnation Revolution in 1974, a military coup so named because there were no shots fired and red carnations, symbolic of socialism, were put into the muzzles of the rifles of the military. The new socialist government pledged a transition to democracy and immediately ended the colonial war, granting independence for Angola and other territories including Mozambique in South-East Africa and East Timor in South-East Asia. This prompted a mass exodus of Portuguese citizens from these countries.

Civil war broke out in Angola immediately after independence in 1975 and became Africa's longest-running conflict. The communist government established by former rebels, backed by the Soviet Union, fought against insurgents supported by the United States. In 1995 the UN sent a peacekeeping force to oversee disarmament and the conflict finally ended in 2003, leaving the country littered with land mines and an economy in tatters. However, since then Angola has developed stability and economic wealth based on oil and diamond revenues.

Jewish Exodus

Against the backdrop of decolonization was a growing conflict between Arabs and Jewish refugees fleeing from antisemitism and unstable countries. Persecution of Jews had been ongoing from the moment Jewish communities first migrated from the kingdom of Israel (in Palestine) into Christian Europe. The Dreyfus Affair (1894–1906), when a Jewish French army officer, Captain Alfred Dreyfus, was framed for treason as authorities covered up for the real culprit, was just one example; the Holocaust from 1941 to 1945 was another (see page 96).

Reacting to antisemitism in the late nineteenth century, the Zionist Organization, led by Hungarian journalist Theodore Herzl, bought land in Palestine and established Jewish settlements there. The Zionists believed that diaspora Jews should return to their homeland in Palestine, a land promised to them by God, and argued that a Jewish sovereign state should be established there. They organized mass migrations to Palestine, raising funds to assist poor and persecuted Jews. During the First World War, worried about Jewish settlements' vulnerability to Turkish forces, the Zionists welcomed Britain's 1917 conquest of Palestine, particularly Chaim Weizmann, a British-educated Zionist who would go on to become Israel's first president.

In 1917 Weizmann helped persuade British Foreign Minister Arthur Balfour to pledge support for a 'Jewish national home in Palestine', causing Jewish immigration to rise. Jewish industry, technology and educational facilities developed. This led to tensions between Palestinian Arabs and Jews, so Britain began to restrict immigration to Palestine in 1930, just as Jews in Germany and Austria were beginning to face a new wave of discrimination. In May 1939, on the brink of a war that unleashed the Holocaust on European Jews, Britain clamped down again on immigration, leading to 'illegal' immigration in which Jews were smuggled into Palestine by Jewish resistance groups.

After the Second World War, Jewish refugees, supported by the USA, attempted to migrate to British-administered Palestine. Britain, conscious of Arab nationalist objections, again restricted the number of immigrants to Palestine. In protest at what it saw as British bias towards the Arabs, the Jewish underground army Irgun set off a bomb in the King David Hotel in Jerusalem in 1946, killing ninety-one people. With mounting tensions, the British submitted the problem to the United Nations in 1947. The UN voted to partition Palestine into Jewish and Arab states with Jerusalem as a shared international zone, a plan accepted by Jewish leaders but bitterly rejected by Arabs. An escalation of Arab attacks was met with more violence by Jewish Haganah paramilitary forces. British troops left the region in April 1948 and on 14 May the independent Jewish state of Israel was proclaimed, a few hours before the British Mandate expired, by David Ben-Gurion, chairman of the Jewish Agency for Palestine.

The next day, Israel was invaded by Egypt, Syria, Lebanon, Transjordan (present-day Jordan) and Iraq in the first Arab–Israeli War (Israel's War of Independence). The Israelis resisted the invasion. By the time of the 1949

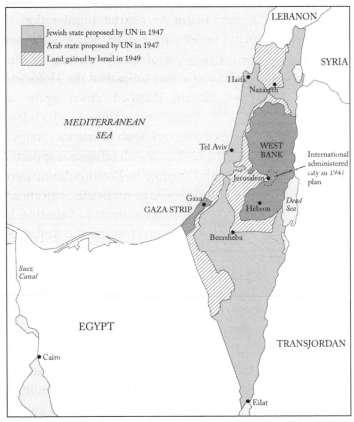

11. *The 1947 partition of Palestine and the 1949 ceasefire agreement.*

armistice, Israel had extended control of territory beyond the 1947 partition boundaries, Egypt had occupied the Gaza strip, and Transjordan had annexed Judea and Samaria. The 700,000 Palestinian Arabs displaced by the war poured into Jordan, Egypt, Syria and Lebanon, where some of the aggrieved Palestinian people formed the Palestine Liberation Organization (PLO).

The new Jewish state of Israel became the focus of mass Jewish immigration from decolonized Muslim North African countries and Arab countries of the Middle East. Jews also came from Egypt, after they were expelled during the Suez Crisis of 1956 (see page 137).

Yom Kippur and Camp David

The Israeli–Palestinian conflict continued with a Six-Day War in 1967 between Israel and its Arab neighbours, who had unified against Israel. The result was a loss of more Arab territory, 600,000 Palestinians in the West Bank living under Israeli administration and the Israeli occupation of the Sinai Peninsula (formerly Egyptian territory), an outcome that was to bring more complications for Israel and more terrorism.

The Arab humiliation of 1967 led to the 1973 Yom Kippur War (named after the Jewish holy Day of Atonement). Egypt and Syria launched surprise attacks on Israeli-occupied Sinai (east of the Suez Canal) and the Golan Heights bordering Syria. The USA under President Richard Nixon gave military support to the Israelis. In retaliation an oil embargo was imposed by Arab members of OPEC on shipments of oil to the USA and Europe, causing oil prices to rocket by 130 per cent and triggering an economic recession in the Western world (see page 107). Again, the superior Israeli army prevailed before the United Nations negotiated a ceasefire. The historic Camp David Accords, signed in 1978 at the US White House by Israeli Prime Minister Menachem Begin and Egyptian President Anwar Sadat, witnessed by US President Jimmy Carter, returned the Sinai to Egypt in exchange for Egypt's recognition of Israel as a nation.

Although peace between Egypt and Israel has held, Palestinian and Israeli relations remain tense and the Arab–Israeli conflict is far from over.

A New Imperialism

The powerful USA, having granted independence to its own colony in the Philippines, had encouraged European powers to dismantle their colonial empires after the Second World War with the objective of opening up trade markets and developing capitalism around the world. The Soviet Union had also supported decolonization, but with the rival objective of spreading communism to regimes in developing countries. During the Cold War (see page 155) these opposing ideologies funded power struggles between communists and pro-Western nationalists.

By the end of the century, Portugal's last remaining colony of Macau on mainland China had been transferred to the People's Republic of China (in 1999) and Britain had transferred the island of Hong Kong to China (in 1997). Hong Kong had been ceded to the British in 1842 after China lost the First Opium War (see page 18) and had developed a free-market economy. As part of Britain's 1997 agreement with China, the island was allowed to retain its capitalist economic and trade systems for fifty years after the handover.

Britain's remaining overseas territories, including Bermuda, Gibraltar and the Falkland Islands, voted to remain as such and today have internal self-governance while Britain looks after their defence and foreign affairs.

The European colonial era was over. Former colonies were left with a mixed legacy of colonial infrastructure, war damage and commercial profiteering. African countries in particular have struggled to recover from their past, but an abundance of natural resources, such as oil, copper, gold, diamonds and rubber, has helped to underpin economic recovery in some.

Many commentators argue that traditional colonialism, involving the physical occupation of overseas territories, has been replaced by a new imperialism (neo-colonialism) of dominant countries taking cultural, economic and social control over economically dependent nations by using capitalist systems of trade and globalization to extend their power and influence.

CHAPTER 7

COLD WAR
CHILL

In 1946 Soviet leader Joseph Stalin said that communism
and capitalism could never live peacefully together, and that
conflict would be inevitable until a communist victory over
capitalism was achieved. Stalin was following the ideology
of nineteenth-century socialist philosopher Karl Marx.

On the other hand, the USA and Western European
nations believed in free-market capitalist economies, free
and democratic elections, and the right of individuals to
acquire property.

From the moment that the first communist state, the
USSR, was established in 1922 (see page 63), proponents
of the two political systems regarded each other with
suspicion, each fearing that the other was trying to destroy
them. At the end of the Second World War this mutual
distrust became a military stand-off as the USA and the
USSR emerged as the most powerful nations in the world:
superpowers with weapons that could destroy the planet.

For decades the world lived under the threat of possible
nuclear destruction, but fortunately, both sides always drew
back from the brink of starting a nuclear war. Instead, they

fought the Cold War by proxy, influencing other countries or intervening in their affairs to gain the upper hand.

Staggering sums of money were spent on Cold War rivalries: US military spending is estimated to have reached $8 trillion in buying military equipment, arming anti-communist groups around the world, researching nuclear or other weapons and fighting the Korean and Vietnam wars. In the Western world the financial drain contributed to the end of the mid-century economic boom, and in the USSR it hastened the end of communism in Eastern Europe.

The Iron Curtain Falls

Soviet leader Joseph Stalin had expansionist ideas that the Second World War helped bring to fruition. In 1939 he forged the unexpected Nazi–Soviet Pact with Germany's Adolf Hitler, which divided Poland between the two countries. As agreed, on the outbreak of the war (see page 81) the USSR invaded Poland soon after Germany's invasion, and they carved up the conquered country between them.

In 1941 Stalin joined the Allies after Germany turned on the USSR, and in 1944, when it seemed that Germany was facing defeat, Allied leaders met in Moscow to discuss the future of Europe. Handwritten notes by British Prime Minister Winston Churchill show an intention to allocate spheres of influence to Allied countries, including the USSR, after the war. But a year later in February 1945, at the Yalta Conference in the Ukraine, Churchill and US President Franklin D. Roosevelt tried to reduce Soviet influence in Poland. Although the conference provided for the United

Nations (see page 103) to be set up and agreed to divide Germany and Berlin into occupied zones, it sowed seeds of suspicion between the USSR and the West.

'Never mind. We'll do it our own way later,' Stalin wrote after the conference to Soviet Foreign Minister Vyacheslav Molotov (whose name was given to bottle fire-bombs). The Soviet leader not only wanted to expand Russian influence, but was also determined to protect Russia by creating a bulwark of communist states between Russia and Western Europe.

In Yugoslavia the resistance, led by communist Josip Tito, did the lion's work of ousting the Nazis and Tito was elected president of an independent federated communist state. Yugoslavia was never dominated by the USSR and

12. *The Iron Curtain between West and East Europe.*

chose to be non-aligned rather than join the Soviet bloc of nations.

Elsewhere, the Soviet Red Army liberated much of Eastern Europe and the Balkans from the Nazis and was welcomed, especially by the many communist freedom fighters. The USSR supported communist parties and helped them run propaganda or intimidation campaigns, so that by 1949 there were Soviet-influenced communist governments in Hungary, Bulgaria, Romania, Czechoslovakia and Albania, as well as in Poland. In the same year these countries were joined by East Germany when the Soviet-occupied zone of that country became the German Democratic Republic.

Winston Churchill declared that 'an iron curtain has descended across the continent'. In response Stalin called him a 'warmonger'.

... And the Wall Goes Up

Nothing symbolized the clash of Cold War cultures so much as the divided city of Berlin with its wall isolating the Eastern zone from the West.

In 1948 the non-Soviet zones of Germany and Berlin, occupied by Britain, France and the USA, were merged into one new state of West Germany. Berlin lay deep within Soviet-occupied East Germany, so Stalin's response was to try to force the Allies out of Berlin completely. He cut electricity supplies and sent troops to block every route into the western part of the city, starving the population.

The only way into West Berlin was by air, and the Allies broke the blockade with what was to become the biggest air supply operation in history. The Berlin Airlift lasted nearly a year, from June 1948 to May 1949, during which time about 1.5 million tons of supplies were delivered before the USSR gave up and lifted the blockade.

This was the Cold War's first stand-off and it set the pattern for the decades to come. The USSR and Western powers never directly came into battle with each other.

In August 1961 the USSR put up the Berlin Wall. The Soviets claimed it was to prevent Western propaganda reaching the East, but their main purpose was to halt the constant emigration of East Germans into West Berlin and the Western world. East German border guards had orders to shoot anyone illegally crossing the wall, and although the total number of deaths is disputed, at least 138 East Europeans died in attempts to escape to the West.

Safe behind its satellite states, the USSR controlled all contact that its ordinary citizens had with the West. Accusations of totalitarianism were justified as the iron fist of the single-party state clamped down on freedom of speech and deported dissidents to gulags, prison camps in Siberia or other inhospitable parts of the Soviet Union.

On the other side, the USA declared itself the champion of freedom. But in its zeal to oppose communism it sometimes supported totalitarian right-wing regimes, for example the military junta in Chile that overthrew the socialist President Salvador Allende in 1973.

Warsaw Pact Unites and Divides

Cold War tensions increased when, in 1955, West Germany was permitted to form an army again for the first time since the end of the Second World War and to join the North Atlantic Treaty Organization. Set up in 1949 by the USA, Canada and ten Western European nations, NATO was a mutual security pact: an attack on any member would be considered to be hostility towards all. It was the first of a web of military alliances that the USA wove around the world to oppose communism during the Cold War. Other countries such as Australia later joined NATO. Australia, New Zealand and the USA also formed their own separate military pact, the Anzus Treaty, in 1951.

The USSR saw the newly militarized Germany as a threat and responded by forming the Warsaw Pact, a defence alliance of East European communist states. Countries that did not align themselves with either military grouping became known as the Third World. The Warsaw Pact allowed Soviet troops to be stationed throughout signatory nations, which caused resentment in some countries.

In Hungary, anti-Soviet feelings came to a head in 1956 with a popular uprising that culminated in a new government deciding to withdraw from the Soviet bloc. This the USSR would not allow, and in November 1,000 tanks rolled into the capital city of Budapest and crushed the nascent revolution. Thousands of Hungarian soldiers and civilians died, and 200,000 fled into Austria.

It was seven more years before another East European state attempted to change its position as a USSR satellite. In 1968 Alexander Dubček, head of the Czechoslovakian Communist Party, introduced what became known as the Prague Spring, a series of reforms including abolishing censorship and allowing freedom of the press. The Soviet response was to occupy the capital city, Prague, stationing tanks in the streets and troops around government or media buildings. Dubček was arrested and replaced, and opposition to Soviet domination was crushed for decades.

American Eagle Flexes its Wings

While the USSR was establishing a communist buffer zone around itself in Eastern Europe, in 1947 US President Harry S. Truman introduced the Truman Doctrine to contain Soviet influence (see page 101): 'I believe that we must assist free peoples to work out their destinies in their own way,' Truman told the US Congress. This policy of containment was tested early in the Cold War in Greece and Turkey.

During the German occupation of Greece in the Second World War, the Greek resistance began an internecine struggle between communists and republicans. Subsequently a civil war began in 1946, with Yugoslavia giving military aid to the communists and Britain supporting the republicans. Struggling with its own postwar economy, Britain had to withdraw its support and the USA stepped in. Its aid was instrumental in the right-wing victory, and Greece became the only Balkan country not to turn to communism.

Britain was also too financially straitened to keep supporting Turkey, which in 1947 was coming under increasing pressure from the Soviet Union to allow Russian naval bases in the Turkish Straits and to give free access through the Straits from the Black Sea to the Mediterranean. Soviet ships began to mass in the region, so the USA sent an aircraft carrier to Turkish waters and provided some $100 million in economic and military aid to Turkey. These confrontations of the Cold War set the stage for the years ahead.

Korea Divides

Korea's fate was determined by other countries from 1910 onwards, when Japan occupied the peninsula as part of its nationalist expansion in Asia (see page 91). At the end of the Second World War Japan was expelled, with the victorious Allies dividing the country along the 38th parallel. North of that latitude the USSR administered the region, while the south was occupied by the USA.

Led by Kim Il-sung, communist North Korea was supplied by the USSR with artillery and tanks, and when the USA withdrew from the southern Republic of Korea in 1950, he launched a surprise attack over the border aiming to unite the country. The South appealed for help to the United Nations, which in turn called on its member nations. Fifteen countries responded by sending military assistance to the area and led by the USA they fought under the UN banner for the first time.

American bomber planes prevented the North from advancing and in a daring move the UN forces, led by US General Douglas MacArthur, landed at Inchon behind the North's lines, breaking the assault before going on the offensive and pressing forward almost to the border with China. This brought a new Cold War power into the conflict. Feeling under threat, the communist People's Republic of China dispatched a massive force of its

People's Liberation Army, which inflicted a major defeat on the UN at Unsan before advancing south.

MacArthur wanted to escalate the conflict with a war of aggression against China, but in a surprise move US President Truman sacked him in April 1951, telling America that it 'would be wrong – tragically wrong – for us to take the initiative in extending the war'.

The following month the Korean War entered a long period of stalemate and negotiations, with the front lines remaining near the 38th parallel. Finally in 1953 an armistice was agreed, formally separating the country, and North Korea gradually took an isolated path to totalitarianism under Kim Il-sung and his heirs.

Spies, Space and Steroids

Cold War suspicions created the age of the spy. Secret agents, double agents and even triple agents were everywhere, including an art adviser to British Queen Elizabeth II, Anthony Blunt, who in 1964 was revealed as a Soviet spy. Secret police in communist countries patrolled for dissidents, and in the USA 'reds under the bed' paranoia led to McCarthyism. This was the name given to a witch-hunt for communists spearheaded by Senator Joseph McCarthy, who in 1950 began to accuse government officials and public figures, such as Hollywood actors, screenwriters and directors, of being subversive Soviet sympathizers. With the help of the Federal Bureau of Investigation (FBI) under J. Edgar Hoover, McCarthy accused thousands of disloyalty, stripping people of their jobs through blacklists and imprisoning hundreds.

It was only when he turned on the military in 1954 that President Dwight D. Eisenhower (a hero of the Second World War) and the US Senate put a stop to his smears. But while McCarthyism was at its height, in 1953, the American couple Julius and Ethel Rosenberg, who had passed information on the atomic bomb to the USSR, were executed as spies.

Cold War competition spread into every area of life. Sporting events became a battlefield, epitomized by the 'Blood in the Water' water polo match between Hungary and the USSR at the 1956 Olympic Games held in Melbourne, Australia. By this point the Hungarian Uprising had been suppressed by the Soviets (see page 160), and tempers were so frayed that players and spectators came to blows.

Success in the Olympics was considered to be so important that East European nations resorted to widespread drug abuse to enhance their athletes' performances. Both sides boycotted Olympic Games because of political events: the USA stayed away from the Moscow Games in 1980 to protest the Soviet invasion of Afghanistan, and the Soviet bloc missed the Los Angeles Games in retaliation in 1984.

Cold War rivalries moved into space as the USA and the USSR sought to prove their technological supremacy. America was shocked when in 1957 the USSR launched the first satellite, Sputnik, and put the first man in space in April 1961 when Yuri Gagarin entered orbit.

Desperate to restore national pride and surpass the USSR in the space race, the following month President John F. Kennedy announced that America would reach the moon. 'I believe that this nation should commit itself to achieving the goal, before this decade is out, of landing a man on the moon and returning him safely to the earth,' he told the US Congress. In July 1969 his ambition was achieved when Neil Armstrong and Buzz Aldrin, exiting Apollo 11, were the first humans to walk on the moon. Kennedy didn't witness it: he was assassinated in 1963. It is still not clear why Kennedy's assassin, Lee Harvey Oswald, committed the deed.

Castro, Che and Cuba

When the Cold War began the USA had the upper hand since it was the only nation with an atomic bomb. This did not last long as in 1949 the USSR developed its own atomic bomb. From then on the two superpowers competed in an arms race to become the greater military threat or deterrent. It was not so much a balance of power as a balance of terror, as both sides worked to create a hydrogen or thermonuclear bomb whose explosion would be about 500 times more powerful than the atomic bomb that was used to end the Second World War. By 1962 both sides were armed with enough of these missiles to potentially wipe out civilization.

The next military goal was to develop missiles with an ever-longer reach. But from 1959, the USA felt itself under threat from a small island in the Caribbean: Cuba.

In 1959 Marxist forces, spearheaded by revolutionaries Fidel Castro and Che Guevara, had overturned the right-wing government in Cuba that had been supported by the USA. Then in 1961 came the Bay of Pigs fiasco when an invasion force of right-wing Cuban exiles, backed by the USA, failed in its mission to capture the country. This spurred Castro to seek the protection of the USSR. Infuriated by a communist regime in its own backyard, the USA imposed sanctions against Cuba, but Castro was still able to send troops to bolster Soviet-aided wars in Angola and Ethiopia. Young, handsome and intense, Che Guevara became a symbol for revolutionary youth throughout the world.

Nuclear Terror: Cuban Missile Crisis

The most terrifying moment of the Cold War came in October 1962 during a 'week that changed the world'. An American spy plane spotted Soviet nuclear missile bases under construction in Castro's communist Cuba, just 150 kilometres (90 miles) from the USA, meaning that the missiles could reach Miami, New Orleans and Washington, DC.

It was a threat that the USA could not accept. In a televised speech President Kennedy announced: 'I call upon [USSR] Chairman Khrushchev to halt and eliminate this clandestine, reckless and provocative threat to world peace and to stable relations between our two nations.'

Kennedy announced an 800-kilometre (500-mile) naval blockade around the island, preventing further Soviet shipments, and warned the Russians that any missile attack from Cuba would incur 'a full retaliatory response' from the USA against Russia itself. He also demanded that the bases be shut down and the missiles removed. USSR leader Nikita Khrushchev responded that the blockade 'constituted an act of aggression'; he refused to back down and Soviet warships carrying weapons continued to sail towards Cuba. At this point Kennedy threatened to invade Cuba, ordering that bomber planes with a nuclear payload be prepared for action. His Secretary of Defense Robert McNamara announced as he walked out of the president's Oval Office: 'I thought I might never live to see another Saturday night.'

Fortunately for the world, neither leader wanted the devastation of a nuclear war. Kennedy commented on the absurdity of the situation: 'It is insane that two men, sitting on opposite sides of the world, should be able to decide to bring an end to civilization.' So after a suitable display of muscles, which had ordinary people terrified, Kennedy and Khrushchev brought the world back from the brink of war and began to deal.

The Soviet warships turned back and the USSR removed its missiles from Cuba in return for Kennedy's promise that the USA would never invade the island. There was another clause to the agreement, kept secret from the American public for twenty-five years to shield the government from appearing weak, that the USA would remove its own nuclear missiles from Turkey, from where they threatened a response to Russian invasion of Western Europe.

These frightening weeks had lasting repercussions. The two superpowers began negotiations that led to nuclear test bans and the leaders installed hotline telephones between the White House and the Kremlin. The threat of a hot war between the world's superpowers was gradually replaced by a spirit of co-operation.

The Cold War Defined in Vietnam

In the First World War conscientious objectors who refused to fight on moral grounds were shunned; in the Second World War they were directed into non-combatant roles. But in the 1960s a popular anti-war movement grew that not only supported peace in general, but specifically opposed the war in Vietnam.

Both a nationalist and a Cold War struggle, the Vietnam War from 1955 to 1975 was the defining conflict of the Cold War. It epitomized the waste of military resources – human losses in this case – in the drive to win the upper hand.

Having forced out its French colonizers, Vietnam divided in 1954 into the communist North led by Ho Chi Minh and the pro-Western South under Ngo Dinh Diem (see page 138). But instead of holding democratic elections as promised, Diem appointed himself president. Worried by the strengthening communist element in the South, the Viet Cong, the USA gave military equipment, advisers and aid to Diem, and in 1964, when a US vessel was fired upon by the North Vietnamese in the Gulf of Tonkin, the USA sent its forces to war.

The following year 100,000 US soldiers were sent to Vietnam, reinforced by troops from Australia, New Zealand and Asia. It became a war of attrition rather than a war for territory. Supplied from the USSR and China through what was called the Ho Chi Minh Trail, the Viet Cong guerrillas could melt into the jungle or merge with the civilian population; even if defeated in a particular area they would just re-emerge from the jungle once the Americans had moved on.

The US response was to sow the countryside with landmines or to bomb from the air. The incendiary chemical napalm, which stuck to the body and continued to burn after it landed, was used even against civilians. The poisonous herbicide Agent Orange was sprayed to destroy the Viet Cong's hiding places but also killed all life in the jungle.

Burning the Draft Cards

Vietnam was the first war to be televised live. The world watched in horror as villages burned, civilians fled and coffins of the military dead stacked up. From its start the war was unpopular with many sections of American society, and protests against it and the military draft formed part of the 1960s' counterculture, with young men burning their draft cards in public. The African-American boxer Muhammad Ali rejected his draft call-up in 1966, saying that he would not go 'to help murder, kill and burn other people to simply help continue the domination of white slavemasters over dark people'. He escaped a prison sentence for avoiding the draft, although he was stripped of his world boxing title.

A year later the North Vietnamese and Viet Cong launched a surprise offensive. It became clear that the USA was far from a victory, and in 1969 the new US President Richard Nixon began a slow withdrawal from Vietnam as well as withdrawing aid, which irrevocably weakened the South.

The last American troops left in March 1973 but the conflict continued as the North pressed forward in

1975, taking the capital city of Saigon in April. The USA evacuated its last personnel with South Vietnamese refugees battling to gain a place on the helicopters. Others formed the first wave of Vietnamese boat people seeking refuge in non-communist lands.

The Vietnam War was a shock for the USA. For the first time in the modern world its military might had not prevailed. According to the US Department of Defense, the war cost $173 billion, a monetary drain that contributed to ending the mid-century economic boom (see page 106). Nearly 60,000 Americans died, while Vietnamese casualties were probably more than 1 million – most of them civilians. In addition, the war cost the American government the support of huge numbers of its own civilians.

A Step Too Far

In the 1970s the Cold War between the USA and the USSR showed some signs of thawing as both sides pulled away from the brink of nuclear war and tentatively explored treaties that signalled the formal relaxation of tensions. US President Nixon visited China and the Soviet Union in 1972, and the first strategic arms limitation treaty (SALT I) was signed later that year. SALT II was signed in 1979, but in the same year the USSR invaded Afghanistan, and Cold War tensions resumed.

Just as the Vietnam War showed that America was not all-conquering, the Soviet war in Afghanistan in 1979 proved that the Red Army was not invincible. Aiming to prop up Afghanistan's communist regime, which was threatened by conservative and Islamic insurgents, the

USSR first sent military advisers, then launched a full-scale invasion, installing a new puppet government.

The Muslim guerrillas, known as Mujahideen (those engaged in jihad or 'religious struggle'), received weapons and money from the USA, Pakistan and Saudi Arabia. When the Mujahideen gained anti-helicopter missiles, the USSR began to lose its air domination of Afghanistan. One of the groups funded by anti-communist countries was the Taliban, which would go on to run an oppressive Islamic regime in Afghanistan and give shelter to the terrorist group Al-Qaeda (see page 195).

The new Republican American president, Ronald Reagan, who took office in 1981, was fiercely anti-communist, calling the USSR an 'evil empire'. He increased military spending, began a new wave of US interference in Latin America such as arming the right-wing Nicaraguan Contras, and planned the Strategic Defense Initiative, a programme of defensive space satellites known as Star Wars. But in the mid-1980s the USSR was in deep economic difficulty. It could no longer match the USA in the arms race or in global influence.

Glasnost and Perestroika

In 1985 Mikhail Gorbachev became the new head of the Soviet Union. Faced with an ageing industrial base, a government that had become corrupt, unpopular and ineffective, as well as the expense of the Afghanistan war, Gorbachev took radical steps that would transform the world.

Hoping to revitalize the economy and develop the USSR into a modern democracy, Gorbachev introduced the policies of glasnost ('openness'), including ending state censorship, and perestroika ('restructuring').

Unable to keep pace militarily with the USA, Gorbachev began to withdraw from Afghanistan and in 1989 the last Soviet troops left the country, leaving a chaotic legacy. Gorbachev embarked on a series of summits with US President Reagan, opening the Strategic Arms Reduction Talks (START).

Confident that Gorbachev would not use military power against them, several East European countries began to think about leaving the Soviet bloc, one more step in the process that would lead to the collapse of the USSR.

Solidarity Shakes Poland

Although capitalist elements in the USA generally tried to control workers' organizations, the USA covertly supported a trade union in Poland. After the Second World War unions had become part of the Communist Party's control apparatus in Eastern Europe. The first trade union in a Warsaw Pact country (see page 160) that was not controlled by the Communist Party was Poland's Solidarity, founded in 1980 by shipyard workers under Lech Walesa. The union's strikes developed into social protests against the communist government, which reacted by banning Solidarity, but its members developed the union into a popular movement calling for social change as well as workers' rights. Because Solidarity also opposed Soviet dominance it was secretly funded by the USA.

Solidarity grew into a political party. In 1989 the communist Polish government had to make concessions and allow partially free elections, which Solidarity won. Lech Walesa was elected president, the first non-communist to govern the country since the Second World War, showing that a workers' organization could change a regime.

Soviet Union Crumbles

The year 1989 proved to be a momentous one, bringing an end to the Cold War. Hungary opened its borders with Austria, there were revolutions in several Eastern European nations, and in November 1989 East Germany abandoned its guard over the Berlin Wall. A symbol of Cold War divisions, the wall was toppled by Berliners from both East and West. In December Gorbachev and US President George Bush declared the Cold War over.

The collapse of East European communism and the dismantling of the Soviet Union happened incredibly quickly. Germany reunified in 1990, the same year in which Lithuania declared independence from the USSR. In 1991 Gorbachev fell from power and his successor, Boris Yeltsin, dissolved the Soviet Union into its original fifteen states with the Russian Federation inheriting the political rights of the central Soviet authority. Suddenly allies, the USA gave Yeltsin its full support in his economic reforms that took Russia from communism to capitalism.

War and Peace in Russia

All was not peaceful, however, in the former Soviet republics. In some cases ethnic divisions that had lasted for centuries flared up into civil wars, as in Georgia and Azerbaijan. Russia itself intervened in the region of Chechnya when the Chechen independence movement was opposed by pro-Russians. The Chechen conflict led to terrorism and retaliatory abuses of human rights by Russian troops stationed in the territory, with the violence continuing well into the twenty-first century.

Although the Cold War was over, nuclear arsenals remained. A new series of SALT saw an agreement on arms reductions in 1991, with further reductions agreed in 1993, 2002 and 2010. From a Cold War peak of more than 30,000 nuclear weapons, today the USA and Russia each have about 1,500 nuclear missiles.

Enter China, Stage Left

Although the Cold War was mainly a confrontation between capitalist USA and communist USSR, China, the other major world communist power, also had a part to play: after the Cold War China replaced the USSR as the only superpower apart from the USA.

China had begun to take a role in world affairs during the Second World War (see page 68), when China's struggle against Japanese invasion became part of the wider global conflict. During the world war, revolutionaries in the Chinese Communist Party (CCP) had forged an uneasy alliance with the right-wing Chinese nationalist government, the Kuomintang or KMT, under

Chiang Kai-shek, but civil war broke out again in 1946. The CCP grabbed military equipment left behind by the Japanese and was also supplied by the Soviet Union. Led by Mao Zedong, who came to prominence during the communists' Long March to safety in 1934–5 (see page 67), the CCP ousted the KMT. In 1949 Chiang fled to Taiwan, establishing the Republic of China there, while Mao entered Beijing and declared the People's Republic of China (PRC). Despite being a thorn in communist China's side, and never formally recognized by the PRC, Taiwan remains independent.

The young PRC received advisers and aid from the USSR, and for a while Mao followed the Stalinist pattern of Five Year Plans and rapid industrialization. He also followed Stalin's system of encouraging communism in neighbouring lands, supporting communists in the Korean War from 1950 to 1953 and in Vietnam's war of independence from 1954 (see page 139). Although Chinese armies did not take part in the Vietnam War, the CCP supplied arms and food to the Vietnamese Marxists and gave support to other communist groups in Asia and Africa. But Mao was no Soviet lackey, and ideological differences brought about the Sino-Soviet Split in 1960.

China was unafraid of international criticism in its dealings with Tibet, first in 1951 when the PRC invaded Tibet, then in 1959 when it crushed a rebellion there and caused Tibet's spiritual leader, the Dalai Lama, to flee to India, and in its continuing refusal to discuss independence for Tibet amid reports of human rights abuses by the Chinese Communist Party.

Internally, Mao's policies included reforms, such as banning forced marriages, building schools and redistributing land to peasant collectives. He also introduced bizarre schemes such as the 1958 Great Sparrow Campaign, an attempt to kill pests and stop sparrows eating rice and grain. But birds eat insects and as the sparrows died, insect pests damaged the crops. Coupled with drought and ill-thought-out irrigation schemes, there was widespread famine between 1959 and 1961. At least 15 million Chinese died.

The Sparrow Campaign was part of the three-year Great Leap Forward, a campaign to increase industrial and agricultural growth that failed miserably. Mao stepped down as head of state in 1959, but remained chairman of the CCP. He soon felt that China was slipping away from his ideology of mass collectives and his next major act was to encourage the Cultural Revolution of 1966–76, unleashing young people in self-appointed Red Guard units to smash anything and anyone they declared was counter-revolutionary or associated with old habits, customs, ideas and culture. Mao was supported by the 'Gang of Four': radical politicians Jiang Qing (Mao's wife), Zhang Chunqiao, Yao Wenyuan and Wang Hongwen.

The Red Guards created a personality cult around Mao. Collected extracts from Mao's speeches and writings published from 1964 as *Quotations from Chairman Mao*, commonly known as the *Little Red Book*, became an object of veneration. In 1967 the Red Guards became so extreme and violent that the army was called to restore public order, and many Guard members were themselves sent for 're-education'.

Taking Centre Stage

While the Chinese Cultural Revolution was asserting a new struggle against 'capitalist thinking', the popular diplomat Zhou Enlai was arranging for China to take a part on the world stage. In 1971 China joined the United Nations, later taking a seat on the permanent Security Council. Zhou entered negotiations with the USA to reduce Cold War tensions, and in 1972 Richard Nixon became the first US president to visit China. It was a major step forward in improving international relations.

China's transformation from a peasant economy to today's global economic giant began after Mao's death in 1976. The Gang of Four were accused of plotting a coup and arrested, while the moderate Deng Xiaoping came to political prominence. He ended the mass collectivization policies of Mao, allowed foreign influence in China and started to experiment with capitalism.

The first, carefully controlled Chinese 'Special Economic Zone' opened in Shenzhen in 1981. There foreign companies were invited to invest in China for the first time, trade rules were relaxed and government restrictions lifted. The economic growth within the special zones was so rapid (China's output doubled in five years) that in 1985 Deng allowed market forces to prevail around the country, encouraging private industry, privatizing state enterprises and welcoming foreign investment.

In 1992 Deng declared that China had a 'socialist market economy' and at the end of the twentieth century this was considered an economic miracle. The country was more prosperous and stable than it had been for centuries. The economy was growing at nearly 10 per cent a year and the standard of living had increased for about 400 million people; there were private millionaires, and imports and exports were flowing across China's borders.

In 2004 China's GDP was more than $1.65 trillion, with $1.15 trillion in foreign trade and foreign investment of $60 billion in the country. Some 300 million people had moved from the countryside to the cities for work.

China's huge modern economy has brought problems: alongside millionaire business owners there are poverty-stricken migrant workers; cities are polluted and deforestation has created deserts in the countryside. Internationally, China is the world's biggest consumer of raw materials and its cheap goods have meant that manufacturing industries in many other countries have declined.

Deng was no social liberal. In 1989 he sent in tanks against democracy protestors, resulting in the Tiananmen Square Massacre, and China's human rights record has often been criticized. As the new economic and military superpower, China experienced a Cold-War-style stand-off with the USA before the century was out, over military manoeuvres near Taiwan.

CHAPTER 8

SPINNING INTO CRISIS

The latter part of the twentieth century was shaped by many crises, though not of the scale of two world wars. While economic recessions, largely the product of high inflation, plagued the developed world in the early and late 1980s and again in the early 1990s, parts of the developing world suffered insurgency, civil wars, famine, genocide and ethnic cleansing.

Influences of Stalinism and the Cold War struggle emerged in Cambodia in the late 1960s, resulting in genocide under Pol Pot's communist regime. Dismantling Soviet Russia and Eastern Europe then triggered the collapse of the Yugoslavian federation in the 1990s and a brutal 'ethnic cleansing'. Ethnic clashes also led to genocidal slaughter in Rwanda. International humanitarian aid was applied in struggling post-colonial African nations, with varying degrees of success.

Industrial disasters made international headlines, including the Bhopal gas tragedy in India and the Chernobyl nuclear catastrophe in the Soviet Ukraine. Instabilities plagued the Middle East, erupting in conflict between Iran and Iraq.

In the USA the moralistic 'War on Drugs' became an example of 1980s Reagan-era 'zero tolerance' policies. It was deemed a failure in stopping the illegal drug trade. Thirty years later, US President George W. Bush would declare a War on Terror (see page 195) as Islamist extremism became a feature of the twentieth-century landscape.

Pol Pot's Genocide

During the late 1960s the Vietnam War would also have consequences for neighbouring Cambodia. The tragic result would be genocide committed by Cambodian communist dictator Pol Pot against his own people, causing the death of 2 million through starvation, execution or forced labour.

Leading up to the genocide, the war in Vietnam (see page 168) had spilled into Cambodia bringing destabilization and civil war. The Khmer Rouge, a Cambodian communist organization led by Pol Pot, had allied with North Vietnam to oppose the government of the Kingdom of Cambodia, which had gained independence from France in 1953.

Pol Pot's forces staged an uprising in 1968. At the time North Vietnam was supplying the communists in South Vietnam through the Ho Chi Minh Trail, which crossed through east Cambodia, and the USA was bombing bases along the trail. When the Cambodian government took aid from the USA in 1970 and allowed air attacks to increase, Pol was given weapons by China and North Vietnam. Many Cambodians supported him, not because they were communist but simply because they preferred the Asian influence of China and Vietnam to America; many were also angered by America's raids that killed Cambodians as well as North Vietnamese.

In April 1975 the Khmer Rouge took the Cambodian capital Phnom Penh, overthrowing the rule of Prince Sihanouk, and Pol commenced a reign of terror. He aimed to create a worker-peasant state and began emptying the cities, forcing the population into rural work camps. Anyone suspected of Western sympathies or of being associated with the previous regime was executed. A Khmer saying went: 'To spare you is no profit, to destroy you is no loss,' and sites of mass executions became known as the killing fields.

In 1978 Pol turned on Vietnam, by then a united, Soviet-backed communist state. In response Vietnam invaded and the Khmer Rouge fled, reverting to jungle-based guerrilla warfare. In a bizarre twist, they began to receive covert aid from the USA and the UK, which saw them as preferable to Vietnam. The UN arranged free elections in Cambodia in 1991, but Khmer Rouge operations continued until Pol's death in 1998.

Island of War

As so often in twentieth-century ethnic conflicts, the Sri Lankan Civil War from 1983 to 2009 was exacerbated by colonial interference. When Britain took over Ceylon in 1802 there was a small region in the north-east of the island occupied by Hindu Tamil people originally from south India, although the majority of the population were Buddhist Sinhalese. Britain brought in more Tamils from India as plantation labourers, swelling the numbers throughout the island.

Ceylon gained independence in 1948, and the following year the migrant Tamils were disenfranchised, as the Sinhalese began institutional discrimination against the Tamil minority. The country changed its name to Sri Lanka in 1972. A Tamil group campaigning for equal rights, the Liberation Tigers of Tamil Eelam (LTTE or Tamil Tigers) was founded in 1976, and the following year a separatist Tamil party won all the parliamentary seats in Tamil areas. Ethnic tensions began to increase, then in 1983 the LTTE launched a war for independence.

Fighting continued until 1987, with a ceasefire enforced by Indian peacekeepers. It did not last long. Needing to suppress trouble at home, the Indian troops left in 1990, having failed to stabilize the region, and war resumed. The Tamil Tigers used assassinations, suicide bombings and massacres, and were labelled terrorists by thirty-two countries.

Government forces were also accused of atrocities such as rape, the killing of civilians and the murder of prisoners. Accusations were impossible to verify since journalists and human rights groups were banned from the north-eastern conflict zones.

In 2008 the government launched a massive offensive, and drove the LTTE back into a small pocket in the north, trapping about 130,000 civilians in the conflict zone. The Tigers were accused of using civilians as human shields by stopping them escaping.

Finally, in May 2009 the LTTE admitted defeat and the long war ended. A semi-autonomous provincial Tamil council was established, but tensions were not over. Backed up by video evidence revealed after the war, the United

Nations accused both sides of war crimes. Reconciliation in Sri Lanka is still not complete.

Ethnic Cleansing Enters the Dictionary

The Yugoslav Wars of the 1990s can be traced to the end of East European communism. The communist Federation of Yugoslavia created after the Second World War was held together by President Josip Tito. But the various Balkan republics and provinces making up the Federation had different ethnicities, languages and religions.

After Tito died in 1980, the Federation continued until strong, centralized communism crumbled in 1989 (see page 173). Nationalists won all the first free elections in 1990 and 1991, and independence was declared in Slovenia, Croatia and Macedonia. As is often the case, there was an economic factor behind some of the nationalism: Slovenia and Croatia were the wealthiest regions and no longer wanted to share their prosperity, while the rump of the Yugoslavian Federation was determined not to lose them.

War broke out in July 1991. In Slovenia, the Yugoslavian army attacked but failed to take control. In Croatia, Serbian militias, helped by the Serb-run Yugoslavian army, began ethnic cleansing (expelling or killing members of other ethnic groups) and took over about a third of the country by 1992, when a ceasefire was negotiated by the United Nations. It held until 1995, when the Croat army attacked and regained Serbian-occupied territories.

In 1992 Bosnia declared independence, but the Yugoslavian army again reinforced Bosnian Serbian militias, who began a siege of Sarajevo in April and started ethnic cleansing elsewhere. The war rapidly descended into one of the worst forms of twentieth-century nationalism: genocide. Although it was supposed to be a UN safe haven, in July 1995 Serbs massacred 8,000 Bosnian Muslim men and boys in Srebrenica.

It was not until August when the Serbs shelled the marketplace in Sarajevo that the UN and NATO reacted with a real show of force, and imposed a peace settlement dividing Bosnia into two.

In 1999 NATO again intervened in the region by bombing Serbia when it brutally suppressed a Kosovan uprising. In 2006 Montenegro split from the federation with Serbia, completing the break-up of Yugoslavia, and in 2008 Kosovo gained independence from Serbia.

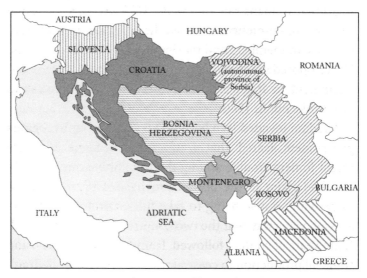

13. Yugoslavian republics and provinces.

The Balkans conflict was Europe's worst since the Second World War. It introduced the horrible phrase 'ethnic cleansing', and shocked the world. Serbian President and war-monger Slobodan Milosevic was one of many who were later charged and convicted of war crimes by the UN.

Dictators from Iran and Iraq

The Middle East during the latter part of the century was no more stable. In Iran, the pro-Western king, or shah, Mohammad Pahlevi, fled the country in 1979 following demonstrations against him. A fundamentalist Islamic, anti-Western regime under the Ayatollah Khomeini took power. Iranian oil production dropped, causing a global rise in prices. When the shah went to the USA for medical treatment Iranians saw this as the USA giving him formal support, and protestors stormed the US embassy in Tehran, taking staff members and marines hostage. In response the USA imposed sanctions against Iran and supplied arms and equipment to Iraq's Saddam Hussein when an Iran–Iraq War broke out in 1980.

Saddam invaded Iran because his Baathist non-religious government feared that Iran's extreme Shiite Islamists might foment trouble among the Iraqi Shiite minority. He also laid claim to the border province of Khuzestan, the underlying motive being to take full control of the Shatt-el-Arab waterway that the two countries used to export oil. Eight years of conflict followed, from 1980 to 1988, causing Iran's oil production to cease almost completely while Iraq's was severely reduced, triggering world recessions.

In 1990 Saddam invaded Kuwait on the pretext he was claiming territory that had once belonged to Iraq, but his real reason was to take control of Kuwait's oil wells. This precipitated the First Gulf War, with the USA leading an international force to push Iraqi troops out of Kuwait by 1991. Many of the retreating army were killed in attacks from the air along what became known as the Highway of Death.

Saddam went on brutally to suppress uprisings by Kurds and other minorities. The world stood by until 2003, when the USA accused Saddam of developing weapons of mass destruction in violation of the ceasefire agreement made in 1991. Leading an international coalition, the USA then launched the Second Gulf War, or Iraq War, invading Iraq and eventually toppling Saddam. He was captured in December 2003 and executed by the interim Iraqi government for crimes against humanity in 2006.

Live Aid

While much of Asia and Latin America developed significantly during the second half of the twentieth century, many post-colonial African countries remained underdeveloped, with civil wars in Sierra Leone (1991–2002), Liberia (1989–96 and 1999–2003), the Congo (1993–4 and 1997–9), Ethiopia (1974–91) and Somalia (ongoing from 1991). War combined with famine in the East African countries of Ethiopia and Somalia in the 1980s and 1990s captured worldwide attention and contributed to the development of global humanitarian aid in the form of food, equipment, training and financial resources.

Ethiopia, occupied by Italy in the 1930s and liberated by British Empire forces in the East African Campaign of 1941, had gained independence by 1944. Anti-government uprisings and war had ensued. In 1974 Soviet-backed military dictator Mengistu Haile Mariam took power, but his state farming system failed, causing severe famine during a drought from 1983 to 1985.

Western powers were reluctant to deal with Ethiopia's socialist regime, which they claimed had compounded difficulties by diverting valuable funds, including aid money, into an armed conflict with neighbouring Eritrea. But media coverage showing emaciated Ethiopians brought in millions of dollars in public donations, as did a campaign by musician Bob Geldof and his Live Aid concert in July 1985, held in London and Philadelphia. The funds saved lives but aid distribution to famine victims was problematic and an estimated 500,000 people died.

Humanitarian intervention was again hotly debated in Somalia's 1990s crisis. An independent republic from 1960, Somalia in the Horn of Africa imploded in civil war in 1991 after its failed socialist administration collapsed. Drought and fighting between rival warlords led to famine in which more than 300,000 people starved to death.

The United Nations sent humanitarian aid to Somalia during a ceasefire in 1992, but supplies were hijacked and aid workers were attacked. With millions at risk of starvation, the USA under President George Bush led an international UN task force to distribute food during the early months of 1993, averting the crisis. Then newly elected US President Bill Clinton scaled down his country's military presence in Mogadishu, the capital, leaving a UN force to restore law and order. A month later, twenty-four UN soldiers were killed in an incident believed to be the work of warlord Farrah Aidid, provoking the UN to hunt him down. Clinton deployed a US assault force to join the hunt. However, the loss of two US Black Hawk helicopters and images of bodies of US soldiers dragged through the streets of Mogadishu shocked America, leading Clinton to withdraw US troops by 1995. The mission to find Aidid had failed.

Lessons learnt in Somalia led Clinton to curtail American involvement in armed humanitarian interventions. In Bosnia during the Yugoslav Wars (see page 183) UN peacekeeper troops were warned to turn the other cheek if fired at for fear of 'crossing the Mogadishu line' – from then on the UN would stay out of civil wars.

Longer-term strategies for helping developing countries included the Fair Trade movement ('Trade not Aid'), set up in the 1960s with an emphasis on assisting producers in the developing world achieve fair trade relations and sustainability. Postwar international organizations such as the International Monetary Fund, the World Bank and the United Nations Children's Fund (UNICEF) also helped countries to develop and combat poverty.

Machete Bloodshed in Rwanda

The United Nations faced further criticism for its failure to prevent genocide in Rwanda in 1994.

This small Central African country, part of the German East Africa colony from the 1880s, had passed to Belgium during the First World War. Both Germany and Belgium had perpetuated a long-held division among Rwanda's population, between the dominant but minority Tutsi ethnic group over the majority Hutu.

Belgium governed through the Tutsi monarchy during the 1950s. In the run-up to independence, tensions mounted between Tutsi and Hutu, culminating in the Rwandan Revolution from 1959 to 1961. Trying to restore order, the Belgians replaced many Tutsi chiefs with Hutu, causing the Tutsi king to flee the country. When Rwanda gained independence in 1962 and a Hutu leader was elected, 300,000 Tutsi fled to neighbouring countries, where some formed militia groups. Their attacks on Rwanda were suppressed and many thousands of Tutsi in Rwanda were killed.

In 1994 the murder of Hutu President Juvénal Habyarimana was blamed on Tutsi rebel group the Rwandan Patriotic Front (RPF). A day later Rwandan army, police and government-backed militias began killing Tutsis around the country and encouraging Hutu civilians to kill Tutsi neighbours with machetes. The RPF fought back, causing Hutus to flood into neighbouring Zaire (now the Democratic Republic of the Congo), Uganda, Tanzania and Burundi, which struggled to cope with millions of refugees. After several UN peacekeepers were killed, the UN cut its force in Rwanda, and those left had to watch helplessly as between 500,000 and 1 million Rwandans were killed (around a tenth of Rwanda's population) during the 100-day genocide. A further 12,000 would die in refugee camps through dysentery and cholera.

Led by Paul Kagame, the RPF took over government and began rebuilding the broken country. Since 2000 Rwanda's economy has grown rapidly.

Rwanda's genocide so disturbed the Western world that it hastened the establishment of the International Criminal Court in the Dutch city of The Hague, which came into force in 2002 and has jurisdiction to prosecute individuals for crimes of genocide, crimes against humanity and war crimes.

Industrial Disasters

Industrial expansion across the world during the twentieth century brought many industrial disasters, from mining collapses to chemical plant explosions. In the 1980s two incidents came to international attention. The Bhopal poison gas leak in India was remarkable for the number of deaths it caused: an estimated 15,000. Chernobyl's nuclear reactor meltdown in the western Soviet Union (now Ukraine), while causing directly no more than thirty-four deaths, was the worst nuclear power plant accident in history and led to fears of increased exposure to radiation, mutations and cancer deaths across Western Europe.

The gas leak in Bhopal occurred at a US-owned Union Carbide chemical factory. During the 1980s the factory was producing a toxic ingredient of pesticides, methyl isocyanate (MIC), while cutting back on safety procedures to save costs. In the early morning of 3 December 1984 a valve broke under pressure and water leaked into a tank of MIC causing a cloud of toxic gas to spread over the city.

Panic evacuation followed but within the first few days 3,000 people had died and thousands required hospital treatment. Compensation from the company was paid to victims in 1989, but for many it was inadequate and lawsuits against the company are ongoing.

The Chernobyl disaster in the Ukraine was sparked by a power surge during a safety test in the early hours of 26 April 1986. This caused an explosion in Reactor 4 and the graphite control rods inside began to burn, releasing radioactive fallout into the atmosphere. Firefighters attempted to put out the fire, but the reactor went on burning for two weeks until it was finally extinguished. Some of the firefighters quickly died of radiation sickness and others fell ill. The nearest city of Pripyat was evacuated and remains a ghost town to this day. Radioactive fallout carried by the wind was reported in Sweden, forcing Soviet leader Mikhail Gorbachev to announce the disaster worldwide. The Soviet states of Ukraine and Belarus were badly affected. Governments of European countries in the path of the fallout ordered crops and livestock in upland areas to be destroyed to prevent contamination of human food.

The Soviet nuclear power industry came under international scrutiny and the incident contributed to greater openness in the Soviet Union, paving the way for glasnost and reforms that would bring about its eventual collapse (see page 173).

War on Drugs

Britain, in its mid-nineteenth-century Opium Wars with China (see page 18), succeeded in protecting its profitable drugs trade, but twentieth-century campaigns against the recreational use of drugs led to prohibition in many countries from the 1960s onwards.

America's 'War on Drugs', a term adopted by President Nixon in 1971, was in response to a growing problem of drug abuse worldwide that was funding illegal trade in heroin or opium from Afghanistan and cocaine from Peru and Colombia worth billions of dollars a year.

The 'war' was really a series of punitive campaigns, domestic and transnational, against the consumption, possession and distribution of illicit drugs. During the 1980s Reagan–Bush era it became a militarized campaign against street gangs. In 1988 the costly Operation Hammer, launched after suburban teenager Karen Toshiba was killed in gang cross-fire, resulted in the arrest of over 50,000 people by 1990. By 1995 the war on drugs had led to the criminalization of a large proportion of African-Americans in communities already suffering social and economic problems of poverty and racial violence.

By 2009 US President Barack Obama's administration had dropped the term 'War on Drugs', deeming it counter-productive, and in 2011 a global commission on drug policy reported that the global struggle against drugs had failed. Drug legalization has been advocated by some groups. Others argue for zero tolerance, citing Sweden, where cocaine use is one-fifth that of Spain, where private drug use has been decriminalized. Sweden's approach focuses on public health concerns and involves harsh penalties, but studies have shown that economic and cultural factors are key in driving drug prevalence, not the harshness of enforcement. The struggle to create a unified drug policy continues.

Terrorism's Ugly Turn

In 2005 the United Nations General Assembly described terrorism as 'criminal acts intended or calculated to provoke a state of terror in the general public, a group of persons or particular persons for political purposes', adding that such acts could not be justified, no matter what ideological, religious, racial or other considerations there were.

Many people would argue that this definition should also apply to the actions of states. Another ambiguity is the truth that one person's terrorist is another person's freedom fighter: Nelson Mandela, who was elected South Africa's first black president in 1994 and who won the 1993 Nobel Peace Prize, was once labelled a terrorist, as were Israeli prime minister Menachim Begin and two senior Irish politicians, Gerry Adams and Martin McGuinness. Che Guevara, the Argentinian revolutionary who became a hero to many left-wingers, was thought by right-wingers to be a murderous terrorist.

Twentieth-century terrorists were driven by differing motivations. Some followed Cold War divisions (see page 155), many were nationalist separatists and some caused terror for extremist religious reasons. At the beginning of the century most terrorist acts were assassinations of prominent people, such as the attack by a Serbian nationalist group on Archduke Franz Ferdinand of Austria in 1914 that precipitated the First World War (see page 36). Over time it became more common for violence to be directed at ordinary people, either randomly chosen civilians or military personnel who symbolized a government.

In the 1960s a counterculture encouraged the growth of anti-capitalist, leftist groups such as the Baader-Meinhof Gang (Red Army Faction) in West Germany. Led by Andreas Baader and Ulrike Meinhof, the group bombed shops, police stations, US bases in Germany, killed a hostage and tried to seize the German embassy in Sweden. Their attacks peaked in 1977, the 'German Autumn', but after a failed hijacking, the gang's surviving leaders committed suicide.

The Baader-Meinhof Gang inspired other terrorists around the world in a decade of terror from 1968 to 1978. Driven into refugee camps by the Jewish takeover of Palestine in 1948 (see page 149), many Palestinian Arabs began acts of terror against the new state of Israel and its supporters in the Western world. The group Black September carried out one of the worst atrocities at the 1972 Munich Olympics, killing two Israeli athletes and taking nine more hostage. The hostages, five terrorists and two German police officers were killed in a botched rescue attempt.

In a world of global media, terrorist acts were headline grabbers, giving activists all the attention they wanted for their cause. The Palestinian struggle influenced revolutionaries from all over the world, including the Japanese Red Army, who killed twenty-six people in a 1972 attack on Lod Airport in Israel.

Separatist Struggle or Religious Reason?

Some separatist groups (religious or ethnic groups that want to separate from the larger or stronger group) committed acts of violence to try to force occupiers from their lands. These included the Muslim Brotherhood that opposed British rule in Egypt in the 1930s, the Jewish Irgun group that from 1936 to 1939 fought against British Mandate rule in Palestine, Basque separatists, the extremist FLQ in Quebec, Canada, and Chechen attacks on Russian targets in 1994 and in 1999. Cold War rivalries after the Second World War meant that sometimes terrorist groups were armed not by criminal gunrunners, but covertly by countries pursuing their own objectives.

Although the Palestinian–Israeli struggle continued to be a major cause of terrorism, by the 1980s some Arab groups were planting bombs for wider reasons. The 1988 Lockerbie bombing, when a bomb on Pan Am Flight 104 blew up over the town of Lockerbie in Scotland, was perhaps partly due to Libya's Colonel Gaddafi wanting revenge for America's actions against him, and the first World Trade Center bombing in 1994 was carried out by Islamic fundamentalists driven by a hatred of the USA.

That hatred would culminate in '9/11' in 2001, when Al-Qaeda members hijacked planes and flew them into the World Trade Center and the Pentagon, killing nearly 3,000 people. The USA's response was to declare a War on Terror that saw the US-led invasions of Afghanistan and Iraq, and operations in Pakistan and elsewhere.

The USA also had to contend with home-grown terrorism when in 1996 Timothy McVeigh, a right-winger who resented the federal government, bombed a federal building in Oklahoma City, killing 168 people.

Bloody Sunday

Terrorism in Northern Ireland had both a religious and a nationalist cause: the Irish Republican Army opposed British rule in Northern Ireland, but as a predominantly Roman Catholic group it often chose Protestant targets.

When the Irish Free State gained independence from the United Kingdom in 1922 (becoming a republic in 1948), the northern part of the island remained in the Union. The majority of the population of Northern Ireland was Protestant and predominantly Loyalist (loyal to Britain), while a minority of nationalist republicans, almost exclusively Catholics, wanted the province to become part of the southern Republic of Ireland. A key date in the 'Troubles', which would last thirty years and result in the deaths of 3,600 people, was 30 January 1972, known as Bloody Sunday, when the British Army fired on civil rights protestors in Londonderry, killing thirteen men; another man died later of his wounds. While the army claimed its troops had been fired at, the unarmed demonstrators saw it as state-sponsored murder.

From then on the Provisional Irish Republican Army (IRA) turned increasingly to terrorist tactics. In 1979 it planted a bomb on the boat belonging to Lord Mountbatten, a cousin of the Queen, killing him, his fourteen-year-old grandson and a fifteen-year-old local boatboy. In other actions the IRA bombed military and civilian targets on mainland Britain and planned an attack on Gibraltar.

Finally the Good Friday Agreement in 1998 brought about a peaceful, political resolution with a power-sharing arrangement. In 2010 an inquiry would determine that the British army was to blame for Bloody Sunday as soldiers had not been provoked by the demonstrators but had opened fire on unarmed civilians.

Although the century ended with a new form of terrorism in Islamic fundamentalism it was seen that long-standing conflicts in regions such as Northern Ireland could be resolved.

CHAPTER 9

THE WORLD IN 2000

The twentieth century closed with a human population of 6.1 billion and an age-old fear among some that the end of the world was coming. The Millennium Bug, a concern that computer systems could not adapt to the new millennium date, turned out to be an unjustified scare story.

Technology had taken us to the moon and by the end of the century had given us personal desktop computers with more computing power than NASA had for the first moon landings. Scientific, medical and technological advances had revolutionized life, and the World Wide Web and mobile phones had transformed the way we communicate, allowing information to spread quickly in a global cultural network. It was the American century, not just because the USA began to dominate politically and economically but also because American culture had permeated nearly every country in the world.

By the end of the century many countries were following America's lead on free trade, increasing the standard of living of consumers by allowing them access to more goods and services at lower prices. However, free trade did not come without risk: increased competition between nations was viewed as a potential source of conflict. Individual countries or trade blocs could impose tariff barriers (protectionism) to engage in global trade wars, or to protect home industries from competition, a pattern going back to the Corn Laws in Britain in the nineteenth century.

Longer Lives, Better Lives

Medicine had come of age. In developed countries, many diseases could be prevented, previously deadly illnesses could be treated, and a good diet together with modern hygiene and routine medical care meant that people lived for longer. Life expectancy at the beginning of the century was just 47 in Europe; by 2001 it had risen to 76.8. In Africa, the average life expectancy in 2001 was 50.5, a clear increase on the 1950 figure of 35.6, but still far behind Europe.

Following the discovery of the double-helix shape of the basic genetic material DNA (deoxyribonucleic acid) in 1953, gene therapies had been introduced and the genetic basis of diseases could be altered. For example, the newly evolved disease HIV/AIDS was identified in 1981, and the virus causing it was pinpointed in 1983. The best treatment for HIV so far is a drug that affects the virus on a genetic level, altering its ability to reproduce.

Reproducing life in a laboratory stepped out of the pages of the *Frankenstein* novel and into reality in the 1970s when Paul Berg's experiments in gene splicing had allowed the transfer of genetic material. During the 1980s a bacterium was constructed that could help clean up oil spills, and genetically modified (GM) crops were launched on a suspicious public in 1994. They found favour with the agricultural industry so GM maize and soy products became commonplace.

In the 1980s methods for growing tissue cultures had developed. The resultant stem-cell research helped treat disease, and artificially reared tissue culture was used to test drugs and grow skin cultures.

Though there were still major challenges, including the problem of microbes becoming resistant to antibiotics, by 1997 the giant steps in health care led American scientist Carl Sagan to say: 'Advances in medicine . . . have saved vastly more lives than have been lost in all the wars in history.'

Casting the Net

The idea of linking computers together in a network had come from various sources in the 1960s: computer programmers were interested in increasing computing power; the US military wanted a communications network that could be used in a nuclear war when a command centre might be knocked out; and academics were interested in sharing ideas.

Computer developers in the UK, France and the USA had worked up the concept of a decentralized system with no central command, all computers in the network being 'equal'. Delivering information in 'packets' over slow-speed telephone lines, several small embryonic systems had developed in the 1970s, including CYCLADES from France, an academic and research network called JANET developed mainly by the US and British post office services, and the large and influential ARPANET sponsored by the US Department of Defense. ARPANET's first link was made in 1969 between two computers; by 1972 there were thirty-seven computers linked to the system, and by 1981 there were 213 'nodes' or different points of access.

In 1974 the word 'internet' had first appeared, short for 'internetworking'. In 1978 the Internet proper began to emerge as disparate networks adopted common systems for transmitting their packets of information (TCP or Transmission Control Protocol) and for organizing the addresses of member machines (IP or Internet Protocol), allowing networks to become linked together.

Weaving the Web

In 1989 British computer scientist Tim Berners-Lee proposed a World Wide Web. Realizing that the Internet would allow people to share information, not just computer-to-computer but computer to every other computer on the network, he created ways in which documents on the net could be linked to other documents in a web of shared information, and be accessed by anyone connected to the Internet.

The three essential technologies he invented were HTML (HyperText Markup Language), which formatted information for the Web; the URL (Uniform Resource Locator), a unique address for Web pages; and HTTP (Hypertext Transfer Protocol), the computer language that allowed Web resources to be transmitted and retrieved. He also wrote the first Web page editor and server programs. In 1990 the first Web page was uploaded.

Berners-Lee wanted data on the Web to be available for all as shared information so did not attempt to patent his invention and he campaigned to keep the Web's underlying codes and data open to everyone. 'You can't propose that something be a universal space and at the same time keep control of it,' he wrote.

He may not have considered himself a revolutionary, but with the World Wide Web he truly revolutionized the flow of and access to information and communications.

Reshaping the World

The World Wide Web allowed quick and easy communication of ideas across borders, giving a voice to individuals and making possible the business website: Internet shopping was an early area to take off on the Web.

Not all the changes were welcomed. Internet giants like Ebay and Amazon began to destroy small, high-street shops in fields such as bookselling by offering discounts and choice that smaller retailers couldn't hope to match.

As telecommunications equipment became faster, it became possible to upload audio and visual material as well as text. Traditional entertainment services were reshaped to broadcast over the Web, and the print publishing industry, from newspapers to books, had to adapt to the new technology, offering its content online or in new audio or ebook formats. By the late 1990s the blogging phenomenon had taken shape, enabling individuals to reach massive audiences without using traditional publishing media at all.

The miniaturization miracle continued. The first laptop computers light enough to be carried around had appeared in the 1980s, and the 1990s saw the price of technology drop. Cheaper computers took the Internet to rural areas of developing countries: by 2003 bicycle-powered computers were being linked to wireless networks in remote parts of Asia and Africa. The new technology took knowledge around the world, transforming distance learning and bringing ideas of freedom and democracy inside totalitarian countries. Internet censorship was introduced in China in 1998, and in North Korea an internal Internet strictly controlled access to information: only a handful of academics or government officials were allowed to access the World Wide Web.

In 1994 the first smartphone was introduced, offering Internet access on a mobile phone. With cameras attached to phones and computers, by the end of the century the stage was set for the spread of popular culture and social networking through sites such as Facebook and YouTube, which were to be launched early in 2004 and 2005.

The last few years of the twentieth century saw globalization explode through the revolution in com-munications and the Internet. Companies, international organizations and governments using computers and global communication networks could receive abundant information more quickly and share it with greater numbers of decision-makers. The acceleration and intensity of interactions changed the way people, organizations and governments dealt with one another.

Dirty and Damaging

Industrialized nations of the twentieth century needed energy supplies and by 1990 Europe was consuming 15 million barrels of oil a day, and the USA alone was using even more: 17 million barrels a day. Of that, perhaps three-quarters were used for fuel: petrol (gasoline), diesel and jet. By 2000 there were 500 million cars in the world.

The oil shocks of the 1970s (see page 107) forced Western nations to try to reduce their dependency on Middle Eastern oil. Northern Europe found reserves in the North Sea and the USA began seriously to develop fracking technology (hydraulic fracturing of shale rock) that was to become widespread and controversial in the following century. Natural gas began to flow from new gas fields in the Middle East. Reliance on fossil fuels again became an issue in the 1990 oil shock when prices rose during the First Gulf War, encouraging big businesses to develop alternative energy sources.

Besides economic issues another problem emerged with using oil, gas and coal for fuel: they produced 'greenhouse gases', which were believed to contribute to global warming and climate change. Ever since the 1850s and the Industrial Revolution we had been burning coal in factories and power stations. A by-product was carbon dioxide (CO_2) along with other greenhouse gases, which modern scientists believed accumulated in the atmosphere like a type of thermal blanket, absorbing heat radiating from the earth and sending it back to warm the planet. Since plants absorb CO_2, deforestation, particularly of the Amazon rainforest, also contributed to the greenhouse gas effect.

In the 1960s it was suggested that the earth was getting warmer because of human activities. Scientists claimed that evidence could be seen in higher temperatures, shrinking glaciers and sea ice, warming oceans, sea-level rises and extreme weather, all of which were measured in the second part of the century. By 2000 the earth was approximately 0.7°C (33.26°F) warmer than in 1900, and the Intergovernmental Panel on Climate Change (IPCC) predicted a temperature rise of between 2°C (35.6°F) and 3.5°C (38.3°F) by 2100. Scientists warned that global warming could lead to floods in low-lying areas and cause serious problems for sub-Saharan Africa and other poor regions with limited resources to adapt to climate change.

Cleaning Up the Act

In 1985 the *Rainbow Warrior*, flagship of environmental group Greenpeace, was sunk in New Zealand by French secret agents before she could set sail to protest French nuclear tests in the Pacific. One Greenpeace member was killed. It was a low point in activist–government relations, and exemplified the way that many states did not acknowledge environmental issues.

With governments slow to act, energy and transport companies denied there was a climate-change problem or that industrialization was its cause, but in 1995 the IPCC stated: 'The balance of evidence suggests a discernible human influence on global climate.'

At first it seemed that the only way to avoid ecological disaster was draconian: to curtail greenhouse-gas-emitting activities. But few people in the Western world were ready to give up their car, or a long-distance holiday, or electricity. And no one in developing countries would give up their ambition to have any of those things.

Fortunately, technology seemed to offer a solution. Although environmentalists had been calling for sustainable, renewable sources of energy for decades, the real impetus for the development of solar panels (widely affordable from the 1970s) and wind farms (the first one opened in the USA in 1980) was the need to find alternatives to oil. The first modern electric car was launched in 1990 and, although controversial, nuclear power was promoted as a cleaner alternative to fossil fuels.

Technologies still under development include hydrogen power storage, synthetic fuels and ways of scrubbing CO_2 from the air, as well as improvements to oil and gas extraction so their supplies last longer.

From Paris to the Future

In 1992 the first 'Earth Summit' meeting was held in Rio de Janeiro, Brazil. A further meeting in Kyoto, Japan, in 1997 introduced the Kyoto Protocol that put limits on the amount of greenhouse gases each signatory nation would produce. Attempts to reduce CO_2 emissions were costly in economic terms and the USA, the world's biggest producer of greenhouse gases, did not sign the Protocol.

However, by 2015 the USA and China, the two biggest polluters, had accepted a new Paris Agreement on climate change, which aims to limit global warming by achieving net zero emissions in the twenty-first century.

Globalization of Trade

Although colonialism during the early part of the century established a global trading system, this was based on accumulation of wealth through a positive trade balance (more exports than imports). The system of free trade (open borders for goods without import tariffs and other barriers) as promoted by the World Trade Organization (see page 104) significantly increased international trade and was adopted across much of the world by the end of the century.

By 2000, trade agreements between pairs of countries were being extended to larger groups. In North America in 1994 a trade agreement between Canada and the USA was expanded into the North American Free Trade Agreement (NAFTA) between those two countries and Mexico. The same year thirty-four countries in North, Central and South America and the Caribbean, excepting Cuba, proposed a wider regional grouping, the Free Trade Area of the Americas (FTAA), negotiations for which are still ongoing.

Other significant trade blocs or regional groupings included the Organization of African Unity, set up in 1963 partly to oppose colonialism and replaced by the African Union in 2002; the Association of Southeast Asian Nations (ASEAN), set up in 1967; and 1989's Asia-Pacific Economic Cooperation (APEC) for Pacific Rim economies.

Borders for People

Another trend of the twentieth century was the opening of borders for people living within groupings of nations, for example between members of the European Union and for travel between New Zealand and Australia. The opening of borders allowed a flow of labour and by 2000 many people were earning a living in places far from their home countries, made possible by modern transport and communications. However, illegal immigration was also a growing feature of the century, particularly to Europe from Africa, to the USA from South America, and to Australia from Asia. Illegal immigrants included refugees fleeing wars or famine and economic migrants looking for employment and better lives.

Immigration was to become one of the biggest topics of discussion in the twenty-first century when conflicts in Africa and in the Middle East led to millions fleeing to Europe in a migration crisis unseen since the mass movements of people after the Second World War.

Shifting Power

At the beginning of the twentieth century European countries ruled by aristocratic elites had been a dominant world force, but over the course of the century Europe's position had declined. After the Second World War the democratically governed USA became the world's first superpower, soon followed by the USSR. Towards the end of the century China emerged as an economic giant with influence on the world stage. The balance of power had shifted, and is shifting still.

Another change over the century involved a move towards supranational groupings, based more on economic similarities than the dynastic groupings of earlier treaties: a change from a world of disparate nation-states to an emerging network of international political, social and economic federations and alliances. These groupings transcending national boundaries may prove to be more permanent, but internal differences were already emerging at the end of the century that could threaten international cohesion. For example, in the European Union the number of migrants seeking to enter Europe was threatening the Schengen Agreement that abolished border posts between some EU countries.

Out with the Old . . . In with the New

Colonialism had flourished, then withered in the twentieth century, as most of the great colonial powers accepted that their colonies had the right to independence and self-rule.

The great ideological experiment that was communism had risen and died in Russia and Eastern Europe. As communism collapsed in the Soviet Union, some businessmen in the new Russian Federation embraced capitalism so enthusiastically that they became the new oligarchs, billionaires on the back of Russia's newly privatized industries. While some former Soviet states have assimilated into the EU, others, such as Chechnya, experienced vicious ethnic clashes.

At the end of the century communism began to evolve into something new in China as the country tried to adapt to the now dominant capitalist economic system.

Inequality and Rights

Communism had arisen as the masses, living in extreme poverty, reacted to an unequal distribution of wealth. Although extremes of poverty greatly diminished in the developed world during the course of the twentieth century, income inequality in wealthy countries like the UK began to increase again in the last decades of the century. In developing countries, extremes of wealth and poverty continued with 20 per cent of the world's population still living without electricity. And while medical technology helped to prolong the lives of people in wealthy countries, some 23 million Africans unable to afford or to access medical treatment at the beginning of the twenty-first century were under a death sentence from HIV. At the end of the 1900s about 6 million people a year were dying of starvation, and in the early twenty-first century 650 million people still did not have clean and safe drinking water.

The concept of human rights that evolved during the century in the developed world served to protect children, women and minorities by law, and war criminals came to be prosecuted by international courts. Two of the most positive features of globalization were the foundation of the United Nations to foster international co-operation, and the speedy response of aid agencies, bankrolled by governments and individual charitable donations, to disasters and human rights abuses anywhere in the world.

A Final Word

In many ways the twentieth century was one of war. Two devastating world conflicts, including the Holocaust, were followed by vicious civil wars, localized military actions and genocide in Yugoslavia and Rwanda. Many of the wars reflected two of the century's disturbing themes: militant nationalism and the increase of terrorism.

As the twenty-first century opened, the sense of optimism and confidence that had been present at the beginning of the century was less in evidence. There were new problems. Many people feared that oil, which had come to play a central role in economic affairs by powering most of the developed world, was running out, while nuclear energy was controversial following the Chernobyl disaster. Many scientists believed that global warming was going to lead to climate change, and terrorism was to take a particularly ugly turn in 2001 with the 9/11 attacks in the USA prompting US President George W. Bush to declare a War on Terror. Nationalism would continue to cause conflicts, for example in the Ukraine, and even the Arab Spring – a movement hoping for democracy and positive change – was to lead to disastrous civil wars in Libya and Syria. There were also dire predictions of economic conflict between the USA, China, India and other emerging nations.

The twentieth century brought security and democracy for many people, and in some countries a standard of living that could not have been dreamt of by our nineteenth-century ancestors. The Internet helped spread ideas, education, news and culture, and the social media explosion that was beginning at the end of the century was to transform the way ordinary people interacted with each other across national borders. New global networks were available to terrorists and other malign interests, but also contributed to the bringing of peace, progress and the promise of a better future to the whole world.

BIBLIOGRAPHY

Alexievich, Svetlana, *Chernobyl Prayer*, Penguin 2016

Bainton, Roy, *A Brief History of 1917: Russia's Year of Revolution*, Robinson 2005

Chalton, Nicola and Meredith MacArdle, *The Great Scientists in Bite-Sized Chunks*, Michael O'Mara Books 2015

Davies, Norman, *Europe: A History*, Oxford University Press 1996

Duffy, N. M., *The 20th Century*, Blackwell 1974

Evans, A. A. and David Gibbons, *The Compact Timeline of World War II*, Worth Press 2008

Ferguson, Niall, *Empire: How Britain Made the Modern World*, Penguin 2004

Figes, Orlando, *A People's Tragedy: The Russian Revolution 1891–1924*, London: Jonathan Cape 1996

Howard, Michael and Wm. Roger Louis (Eds.), *The Oxford History of the Twentieth Century*, Oxford University Press 1998

Howe, Stephen, *Empire: A Very Short Introduction*, Oxford University Press 2002

Kershaw, Ian, *To Hell and Back: Europe 1914–1949*, Penguin 2016

Lowe, Norman, *Mastering Modern World History*, Palgrave Macmillan 2013

MacArdle, Meredith *The Timeline History of China*, Worth Press 2007

MacArdle, Meredith, Nicola Chalton and Pascal Thivillon, *The Timechart History of Revolutions*, Worth Press 2007

Marr, Andrew, *A History of the World*, Macmillan 2012

Massie, Robert K., *Dreadnought: Britain, Germany and the Coming of the Great War*, Vintage 2007

National Geographic Eyewitness to the 20th Century, National Geographic Society 1998

Nicolson, Colin, *Longman Companion to the First World War: Europe 1914–1918*, Routledge 2001

Overy, Richard, *Collins Atlas of 20th Century History*, Collins 2005

Overy, Richard, *20th Century*, Dorling Kindersley 2012

Overy, Richard, *The Dictators: Hitler's Germany, Stalin's Russia*, Penguin 2005

Pakenham, Thomas, *The Scramble for Africa*, London: Abacus 1992

Taylor, A. J. P., *The Struggle For Mastery in Europe 1848–1918*, Oxford University Press 2001

Tuchman, Barbara, *The Guns of August*, Penguin 2014

Tuchman, Barbara, *The Proud Tower*, Macmillan 1980

INDEX

Page numbers in italics indicate maps.

INDEX